from Hiroshima to the Hague
a guide to the World Court Project

from Hiroshima to the Hague

A guide to the World Court Project

By Keith Mothersson

International Peace Bureau 1992

From Hiroshima to the Hague

International Peace Bureau
41 rue de Zurich
CH-1201 Geneva
Switzerland
Tel + 41-22-731-6429
Fax + 41-22-738-9419
Layout: KCD Graphics, 37 Wordsworth Rd, Salisbury SP1 3BH UK
Printing: Sarsen Press, 22 Hyde Street, Winchester, Hants, UK

Cover photos:

(i) Hiroshima victim. This 21-year old soldier was 1 kilometre from the hypocentre of the Hiroshima bomb. The photo was taken by Konichi Kimura, two hours before the soldier died of radiation sickness, 28 days later.

(ii) The Hague

ISBN 92-9123-002-2

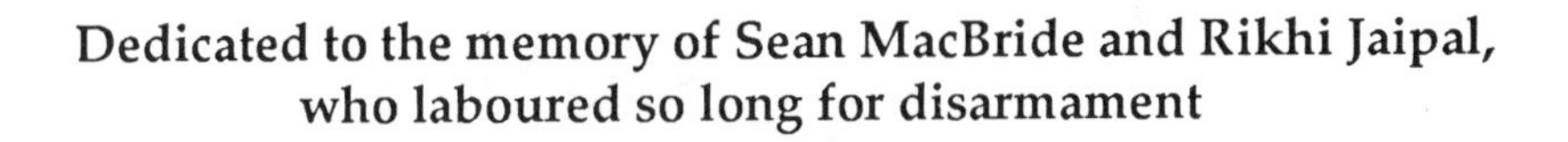

Dedicated to the memory of Sean MacBride and Rikhi Jaipal,
who laboured so long for disarmament

'The time has come to found a movement of political action
that will impose international law standards on the nuclear powers
and bring the people of the world some hope of peace and justice.'

Prof Richard Falk, speaking at Nuremberg, 1983

From Hiroshima to The Hague

Contents

Introduction

In the latter years of the 19th century the early pioneers of the IPB - the world's oldest and broadest international peace federation - gathered together at their Universal Peace Congresses to proclaim and debate the gospel of peace. Foremost among their demands was the insistence that structures of international law and arbitration be created and put to work in order to provide an alternative to war as an instrument of conflict resolution between states.

Now in its Centenary year, the IPB continues to stand for these basic principles. We support - albeit critically at times - the role of the UN in peace-keeping, in the promotion of disarmament, and in its efforts to tackle the root causes of conflict. Above all we are committed to the application of international law to the manifold dangers of weapons of mass destruction. Our late President, the Irish statesman and Nobel Peace Laureate Sean MacBride, devoted much of his later life to arguing for a total ban on nuclear weaponry, on the basis of legal principles dating back to the Hague Conferences of 1899 and 1907 - which IPB had itself helped to initiate - and earlier.

The World Court Project, whose aim is to secure an Advisory Opinion from the International Court of Justice on the legal status of nuclear weapons, is a further expression of MacBride's pioneering vision. It offers a new and exciting opportunity for the concerned public across the world to apply fundamental legal and human values to the question which must still - despite the ending of Cold War hostilities - rate as the most dangerous peril facing humanity as a whole.

The threat of nuclear proliferation is currently much exercising the minds of the military, the scientists and the politicians in the West. However it is striking how one-sided the debate remains. 'Their' arsenals are dangerous, destabilising, accident-prone, out of control. 'Ours' by contrast are reliable, protective, trustworthy and utterly essential. The international law perspective - especially when seen fully in its environmental and human rights dimensions, as well as in terms of the law of war - suggests a way out of the impasse between North and South, nuclear haves and have-nots. This impasse threatens to block, not just the renewal of the Non-Proliferation Treaty in 1995, but the whole range of multilateral anti-nuclear measures we need so urgently.

Law is no panacea. It is an area of struggle between the powerful and the unpowerful, a struggle over social values and meanings. As such it is ultimately a political as well as a technical process. Despite the growth of international institutions and the apparatus of inter-state regulations which chip away at national sovereignty, might still acts as if it is right, and we have the absurd situation where biological (and soon chemical) weapons are banned explicitly but the far more dangerous nuclear ones are not.

There can therefore be no guarantee that the ICJ will return the Opinion we believe in all good faith it should. There is much hard work to be done by the peace movement both before and after its verdict is heard. But I am convinced that the prospect of finally outlawing nuclearism offers an extraordinary ray of hope in a gloomy and cynical world. If carried through with the necessary determination it will prove a stunning victory for a new alliance of citizens' organisations and anti-nuclear governments.

Keith Mothersson's stimulating text combines thorough exposition for the non-specialist with solid argument and original, even visionary, ideas. It does not claim to be 'the official guide' to the Project - there are too many different points of view within the network for that. Rather it represents the accumulated understandings of an independent scholar-activist who has devoted himself to this particular cause over the past several years.

I am extremely grateful to Keith for tackling this daunting task with such characteristic energy, despite the pressure of deadlines. Thanks also to David Head for his thoughtful editorial work and to Kate Cameron-Daum for generously contributing the layout. Comments received from lawyers in IALANA and others in the WCP network were most helpful. A previous draft put together by Sean Byrne, Wibert Quintana and Rainer Santi also proved to be useful source material for the present work. We are grateful to them all and to a variety of financial contributors for helping this volume to reach the public.

Colin Archer, Geneva April 1992

The IPB symbol

Nagasaki; Afternoon, 10 August 1945 Photo: Yosuke Yamahata

Preface

The nuclear weapon should have been banned after its first use in Hiroshima, or certainly after the knowledge that its use in war could result in consequences that would pose a general threat to humanity. But that did not happen, because the military mind, which is far from being the monopoly of the military man, had taken over and, setting aside moral and legal implications, found a questionable reason for keeping the nuclear weapon. The military necessity for this weapon is said to be in its quality of deterring potential enemies from aggression with the threat of its use against them.

The nuclear manner of preserving peace through the force of terror is not free from risks. On the contrary it depends for its success on the very creation and escalation of unacceptable risks. Playing games with the fate of humankind in this fashion has given us all a profound psychological shock and we have to perform many a mental summersault to live with the nuclear weapon. We live in fear of our own extinction while preparing for the extinction of our enemies by it. Such a state of existence causes a hardening of the heart and a state of mind that is continually at war and produces concepts like nuclear deterrence that give a rational appearance to an irrational process.

To the normal mind however, this apparent rationality is riddled with paradoxes. The foremost paradox is that the nuclear weapon is rationalised as a 'peace-keeper', despite the fact that its use would harm humanity beyond recovery. Secondly, its non-use is dependent on a so-called stable balance of terror. Terror does not induce balance or stability, but such is the jargon of nuclear weapons that language is dislocated into meaning other things.

Another paradox is the possession of nuclear weapons by a few States, and them being denied by Treaty to the majority of States on the ground that proliferation by them would be much too dangerous. This fundamental discrimination can be removed only by a universal ban on nuclear weapons.

There is yet another paradox. Having prohibited the majority of States from acquiring nuclear weapons, there has been no follow-up to ban their use. This contradiction is necessary and is maintained by the few States that have nuclear weapons and intend to use them in the event of their failing to deter whatever they were meant to deter.

The use of nuclear weapons by them is considered permissible, because it is claimed that a State may do whatever is not expressly prohibited by Treaty and until now nuclear weapons or their use have not been specifically banned by Treaty. It is not serious of these States to insist that there should be a Treaty expressly banning nuclear weapons and their use, when they are themselves opposed to signing such a Treaty, a draft of which is before the UN.

There are several recognised sources of international law that have the effect of outlawing nuclear weapons. The International Association of Lawyers against Nuclear Arms - and also the following pages - present ample evidence that the use of nuclear weapons would be a violation of international law and a crime against humanity. The UN General Assembly with massive majorities has made declaratory pronouncements to the same effect, which have unquestionable moral authority.

However, this majority view is not shared by several NATO countries, which apparently prefer to rely on nuclear weapons to safeguard their national security. There is thus a dispute between NATO and the majority of UN members in regard to nuclear weapons and their use. It would be perfectly proper therefore for the General Assembly to resolve this dispute by seeking the advice of its principal judicial organ, the International Court of Justice, on the use and threat of use of nuclear weapons.

The primary aim of the most important international Treaty, the UN Charter, is the safeguarding of successive generations from war, and that aim is in danger of subversion by the nuclear weapon. The formidable paradox of nuclear deterrence is that the danger of its failure becomes apparent only when it is too late to avert it.

The defence of humanity must spring from the minds and actions of ordinary people. The impact of non-governmental opinion has already given international politics a human face through various campaigns which are the essential building-blocks of the future of humanity.

Unfortunately the threat to humanity does not seem to matter in the particular view of reality of the States with nuclear weapons. A psychic numbness afflicts all governments when they are faced with the future of the human race. In the circumstances it is clearly necessary for a higher forum such as the World Court or a Special World Tribunal to advise on today's problem of problems, the legal requirements for ensuring humanity's survival in the nuclear age.

The underlying question is the paramountcy of humanity's right to survive vis-a-vis the right of nation States to safeguard their national security with nuclear weapons.

Rikhi Jaipal served for many years as India's Ambassador to the UN in New York, was Secretary-General of the Conference on Disarmament and Vice-President of the IPB. He died in late 1991. This preface was adapted, with few changes, from a talk he gave at the 1988 IPB Annual Conference in Sydney.

Part One: Peace through Law?

A symbol depicting justice at the entrance to the Peace Palace, home of the International Court of Justice (ICJ), at The Hague in the Netherlands. Opened in 1978, it holds the offices of the Judges of the Court.

UN photo:154369/P. S. Sudhakaran

1. Law, morality and politics

The last few years have seen a growing interest in the law on the part of peace movements in many parts of the world (1). But many remain sceptical that the law really can help us. They assume that any laws which States agree amongst each other will merely be conspiracies against the common welfare of ordinary people. This impression is strengthened when we see the most powerful nation preaching the sanctity of international law to Iraq, while cynically manipulating the UN and riding roughshod over the Charter on numerous counts.

Yet just as a three-legged stool is more useful than one with one or two legs, so we should try to co-ordinate the moral, political and legal dimensions of peace work - to mention only three of its many dimensions.

Morality First? Especially in nuclear countries, some peace activists have tended to leave the legal/political field to the government, retreating instead to a position which emphasises the primacy of each person's own conscience. Although everyone must indeed put their conscience first, this approach can sometimes lead to excessive self-righteousness which isolates us further from those we are trying to reach. After all, the idea (central to international humanitarian law) of not attacking defenceless people is not our own private moral invention, but rather a value which most people take for granted in most areas of their lives.

So the moral ground on which we take our stand against nuclearism is not just ours, but that of our society already. Moreover these key moral rules have already resulted in theoretically binding laws and treaties. At least so far as anti-nuclear peace work is concerned, it is unnecessary and counter-productive to counterpose morality or 'God's law' over against politics and 'human laws'. Because it is indeed a spiritual and moral issue we insist on the law being applied and all political obstacles to the rule of law being removed. And if we blockade nuclear bases we shall surely do so as law-enforcers, not as any kind of law-breakers (2).

Politics First? Some of us concentrate on working through the political system for a change in government policy. But this also tends to become sterile if pursued in ignorance of the law and in opposition to legal and moral strategies. Those who say 'Politics First' often think of the law as a trap or a club used by those in power to defend their perceived interests. There is some truth in this view. But it ignores the role that moral appeals and discussion about 'the law' play in political debate and hence in creating election-winning majorities.

ROLE OF LAW IN SOCIAL PROGRESS

We face the challenge of developing remedies for government practices which no longer reflect accepted norms of morality and legality...The law alone will not [resolve society's greatest problems], just as the law would not, by itself, have brought an end to the divine right of kings, slavery, child labor, exclusive male suffrage, racial discrimination or the Vietnam War. **But social progress with respect to these and many other issues would not have occurred without the intervention of legal principles in the political debate, or the confirmation of changing values in the form of legal principles.** So too, in the context of the nuclear dilemma, lawyers and legal principles should lead the way in forging consensus, this time among peoples divided by culture and geography, yet united by common interest in continued survival and world peace.

- Statement by the U.S. Lawyers' Committee on Nuclear Policy, 1990, p 35, emphasis added. (3)

History may be largely the product of power-politics, economic interests and force, but all such activities are clothed in language and pursue some or other idea of the good, the valued, the attainable. The status quo is never just 'brute facts' and 'hard reality' with no accompanying symbolic webs of meaning and counter-meaning. 'Getting power' is not usually like grabbing a machine-gun; nor is 'nuclear disarmament' like taking someone's gun and breaking it. But **what we can take away is the legitimacy** surrounding their nuclear poison-scattering devices. By a world-wide campaign to confiscate and reverse the legal meanings surrounding these devices, we can create conditions in which eventually 'the boys' hand in all of their lethal 'toys' worldwide.

So if power and oppression are not just physical, then neither is 'the law' just one thing with a single finished function. It is also the people's right (in French: *droit*), **a collective shield** painfully constructed struggle by struggle, an arena in which injustice can be contested. Sometimes, when political channels are blocked and moral appeals fall on deaf ears, it is the only way people have to argue back. Think of the victims of Bhopal.

The existing legal system is always a compromise between different interests, values and ideologies. Of course in the present world order the law often fails to correspond with justice, but it cannot fulfil any useful human function (even for the rulers) if it cuts completely its umbilical connection with 'natural law' (4), morality, reason and the basic values most of us learn at our mother's knee: 'do as you would be done by', 'live and let live', 'no bullying'.

Even elite nuclear brotherhoods usually feel compelled to claim a legitimate place in the constitutional order. They disguise their projects in a patriarchal language of 'protection' of women, children, old people and others the nuclear elites in fact exclude and menace: an improbable hypocrisy that gives us our chance. For if it is difficult to believe them when they promise to respect legal limits in conventional war, it is impossible to squeeze the brutal square of nuclearism within the life-protective circle of true law. Not only have the nuclear powers forgotten to pass laws enabling genocide, they have even felt the need to go in for Conventions and Statutes preventing it. That is the fault-line where we can insert our lever, to expose and exacerbate this contradiction.

So let us be wary of the limits of the Law, but not over-cynical. When Brezhnev signed the Helsinki Final Act of 1975 he may have calculated that a little lip-service to 'Human Rights' was small price to pay for secure borders and better relations with the rulers of the West. But the Soviet dissidents saw their opportunity. Unofficial 'Helsinki monitoring groups' began to mushroom which the authorities often impeded but dared not crush, on account of their links to the official Helsinki Review process.

This Handbook is written in the faith that it may be possible to recover and secure our civilian rights to non-combatant immunity, to which even the nuclear nations paid lip service in the Geneva Conventions. It hopes for a global *'Geneva from below'* to complement *'Helsinki from below'*, which pushes the politicians and diplomats to realize the enormous potential for peace still surviving at the heart of international law and in the core of the UN system, of which the ICJ is a part.

'Geneva from below'. Aerial view of the Palais des Nations, housing the European Office of the United Nations. UN photo: L. Bianco/ARA

LAW AS COMMON SENSE

Civilized law is a common denominator of common sense, a social bond which permits each person to live uniquely and at peace. It is not passed down from on high but grows naturally out of ordinary human need and perception. Murder is not a crime because we are told it is, but because we know it is. 'Thou shalt not kill' is present in the human bloodstream, felt in heart and mind, in every part of the world.

- from p.1 of the brilliant and passionate *'Humanizing Hell: the Law v. Nuclear Weapons'* by George Delf, a former Secretary- General of the International Peace Bureau.

2. Peace through law - a historical perspective

The Law of War and Peace has two different strands. What theologians and jurists have called *jus ad bellum* is concerned with rules about going to war; in a wider sense it includes negotiation and decision-making to settle disputes without resort to force; *jus in bello* covers rules for how wars should be fought once entered into. In this section we look at efforts people have made through the centuries to use the law to check violence and to secure peace in a broad sense.

Contrary to many people's assumptions, nearly all indigenous societies have had some or other rules about resolving disputes, declaring hostilities and the conduct of hostilities. These include no sneak attacks; no fighting at night or on holy days; no killing if wounding will do, no wounding if scaring will do; no over-reacting to minor provocations (5).

Scholars of the origins of the law of war have traced how similar concerns have come down to us through all the main world religions (6). To take only two examples:

* in Islam: by the eighth century of the Christian era Al Shaybani had written a treatise on international law and Caliph Abu Bakr was forbidding his warriors to harm women, children and other non-combatants (7);
* alongside a minority pacifist strand, mainstream Christendom evolved a fanatical, militant ethos which theologians sought to control through a series of tests which rulers were encouraged to apply before taking up arms (8):
  - had there been a great wrong?
  - had other ways of vindicating important rights and principles been exhausted?
  - was there good hope of victory?
  - would the evil eliminated outweigh the evils created in the process?
  - would it be possible to ensure that the wrong people didn't suffer?

These 'Just War' criteria influenced the Dutchman, Hugo Grotius, and other European scholars who founded modern international law in a period of revulsion against the ideologically-fanned horrors of the Thirty Years War (1618-1648).

Unfortunately it is a common feature of all the patriarchal codes that the rules tend to apply only so far. Beyond the limits of civilization were 'barbarians', 'pagans' and 'savages' against whom anything was deemed acceptable. Nowadays things are different in theory and the distinction between 'civilized' and 'uncivilized', 'cultured' and 'uncultured' peoples finds no place in the International Humanitarian Law of Armed Conflict.

Even so, during wars racist attitudes constantly surface at all levels of command (9). If frightened soldiers are often prepared to kill soldiers and civilians rather than 'take any chances', the thinking of commanders blinded by the righteousness of their cause differs only in scale. The official rationale for Hiroshima and Nagasaki was 'saving Allied lives'. Even in its own unchivalrous terms the argument is racist - since it discounts the lives of the 40,000 Korean prisoners and forced labourers who also perished alongside Japanese civilians (10).

In 1859 a young Swiss businessman happened to find himself stranded and appalled amidst the carnage of the Battle of Solferino. On his return to Geneva Henri Dunant started a group which grew into the Red Cross and Crescent movement. From an original concern with helping wounded soldiers a series of subsequent Geneva Conventions have sought to protect other categories of non-combatants from attack (11). Alongside this 'law of Geneva' another strand of international law has evolved called the 'law of the Hague'. This has focused on trying to ban certain particularly inhuman categories of weapons and ways of waging war, most notably in the *Declaration of St Petersburg* of 1868 and the *Hague Conventions* of 1899 and 1907.

A third important current of concern was to prevent wars occurring in the first place. Two *Conventions for the Pacific Settlement of Disputes* resulted in agreements to pursue various forms of third-party resolution of disputes, and the creation of the Permanent Court of International Arbitration at the Hague. Founded in 1892, the International Peace Bureau (IPB) was active in promoting these diplomatic conferences and in 1910 received the Nobel Peace Prize for serving as a channel of communication between Governments and the peace movements. After World War I, IPB worked with the Society of Friends to support the League of Nations, to ban gas warfare and for the *General Treaty for the Renunciation of War* of 1928. This also committed the participants to the peaceful settlement of 'all disputes or conflicts of whatever nature or whatever origin they may be which may arise among them'.

Although this Treaty, known as the *Pact of Paris,* failed to prevent World War II it influenced the definition of Crimes Against Peace in the Nuremberg Charter. Both in the West and the Far East, the Nuremberg and Tokyo tribunals were criticised for representing 'victor's justice' using retroactive legislation against only the crimes of the vanquished. Thus the Japanese who supposedly endangered prisoners of war (POWs) by siting their camps near military targets were found guilty, while those who fire-bombed the centres of Tokyo, Hiroshima, Nagasaki and other cities were hailed as national heroes (12). In the West it has been almost impossible to mention, let alone prosecute, the area bombing of Dresden (13), the rape of Berlin and the quasi-murder of a million POWs from deliberate exposure and artificially-engineered shortages in American and some French POW camps in 1945-46 (14).

Such double standards were to bring the cause of international law into disrepute and to create potent breeding grounds for nationalist revanchism. However once the UN had unanimously affirmed the principles of the *Nuremberg Charter* and Tribunal in 1946 and again in 1950, the *Nuremberg Principles* were put on a different forward-looking basis and can serve as potentially universal, preventive instruments with which to realize the unfulfilled promise of Nuremberg.

Law and Peace in the era of the UN

With a Charter full of ringing phrases about peace, justice and human rights, the founding of the United Nations in 1945 raised great hopes for a world without war. Since late-nineteenth century Russia, no nation had been more associated with the idea of compulsory third party settlement of disputes than the America of Franklin Roosevelt. Yet by 1946 it was the US under Truman which itself undercut the new world order it had done so much to bring about. It announced that (like its new Cold War adversary) it would reserve the right to decide which disputes fell within its domestic jurisdiction and which within the jurisdiction of the new International Court of Justice which had been set up in the Hague to replace the old League of Nations Court.

Other states took their lead from this 'Connally Reservation' and 'the whole system of states remained unready to fulfil the promise of the Charter' (15). Other defects in the post-war order have been excessive privileges for the 'Big Five' Allies, their unwillingness to cede power to organs they cannot control and the unprincipled use of the veto system. Among the results have been:

* worsening global economic injustice, ecological devastation, preventable disease and starvation in many areas of the world, wars, massive arms build-ups and exports;
* illegal 'destabilisations' and 'interventions' by big powers who have also cynically shielded the invasions and human rights abuses of certain client states, e.g. in Palestine, East Timor, Ethiopia;
* a chronic nuclear arms race (or 'chase') which still continues in qualitative terms ('Star Wars') amidst ever greater dangers of 'horizontal' proliferation;
* the betrayal of the world community over far-reaching promises to pursue nuclear disarmament contained in the 1963 *Partial Test Ban Treaty* (PTBT), the 1968 *Non-Proliferation Treaty* (NPT) and renewed three times at the UN Special Sessions on Disarmament;

Hence it is hardly surprising that progressive people in many countries and movements grew cynical about the effectiveness of national and international law and the potential of the UN system, perhaps preferring to put their faith in 'Politics first' (Marxists) or 'Moral force' (Western interpretations of Gandhi). This disconnection of morality, law and politics is yet another wound inflicted on us by the nuclear age.

Signs of hope

Yet for all this, the precious legacies bequeathed to us by earlier generations of progressive peace people, lawyers, feminists, anti-colonialists, etc still survive. Although applied unevenly, the principles of 'self-determination', 'non-interference in internal affairs' and 'equal rights of men and women and of nations large and small' contained in the UN Charter have continued to be used by those struggling against imperialism, racism and sexism around the world, e.g. in the ICJ rulings against Apartheid in **Namibia** in 1972, and against US-sponsored terrorism in **Nicaragua** in 1986.

The increase in nuclear tension around 1980 resulted in an upsurge in peace movement militancy, some of which began to be expressed as activities to uphold and enforce the law:

* In the Netherlands 20,000 plaintiffs took the government to Court for its decision to allow Cruise deployments in violation of international law (16).
* In Canada a citizens coalition, *Operation Dismantle*, applied to the courts for a ruling that government permission for US cruise missile tests would make war more likely and hence endanger the constitutional right to life (17).

* In the USA, Germany and elsewhere civil resisters began to couple direct action against physical manifestations of the nuclear machine with legal self-defence based on the criminality of nuclearism under international and hence also domestic law - with several of these 'necessity defences' resulting in acquittals (18).
* In Germany a *Tribunal against First Strike and Mass Destructive Weapons* was convened in Nuremberg at the instigation of Petra Kelly and others in 1983 (19). In 1987 over 20 members of Judges and State Prosecutors for Peace blockaded the American Pershing 2 base in Mutlangen with the support of hundreds of other members, expressed in a full-page declaration in the country's most prestigious newspaper.
* In Japan and Belau citizen groups have organised numerous rallies, tribunals and petitions in defence of their countries' anti-nuclear constitutions.
* In New Zealand a dynamic popular movement first achieved a nuclear-free government policy, then had it enshrined in law in the 1987 *NZ Nuclear-Free Zone, Disarmament and Arms Control Act*, to which even the current National government remains (on paper) committed.

NZ Nuclear Free banner at the UNSSOD III March, New York, June 1988

* In the UK repeated efforts have been made to get the courts to restore the rule of law in this area of national life (20), and leaflets have been openly distributed encouraging military personnel to refuse to obey illegal nuclear commands (21);

In January 1985 a *Nuclear Warfare Tribunal* was convened in London by IPB, Lawyers for Nuclear Disarmament and a wide spectrum of religious, political, trade union and professional groups. The distinguished members of the Tribunal recommended:

> *'the initiation of an effort to obtain an Advisory Opinion of the International Court of Justice on the status of nuclear weapons, strategic doctrines, and war plans' (Recommendation 7.5)*
>
> *'Governments of non-nuclear weapon states have a particular obligation to their citizenry to pursue all lawful and political means available in international society, including recourse to the International Court of Justice, to secure compliance with international law; governments that opt for a policy of permanent neutrality have special legal standing to take action against plans and preparations for nuclear war.' (Judgment Implication 1.3)*

Meanwhile the concerns of indigenous peoples, ecologists and 'green' public opinion were finding expression, however tardily, in a series of international agreements to protect the Environment. This 'common heritage of all mankind' demonstrated the interdependence of nations in ways never envisaged in earlier centuries of unrestrained state sovereignty (23). Increasing detente in the second half of the 1980s saw a rebirth of international confidence in the UN and its ability to solve conflicts through peaceful means. President Gorbachev called for a law-ruled world community of law-ruled nations and appealed for a nuclear-free world by the year 2000 (24).

At their Hague conference in June 1989, the Foreign Ministers of the Non-Aligned Movement (NAM), called for a *UN Decade of International Law* (UNDIL) which would work towards universal acceptance of the compulsory jurisdiction of the World Court. This latter goal, a longtime aim of the World Federalist movement which lobbied hard for its adoption, was omitted in order to secure the support of the West when the proposal came before the UN General Assembly on November 17th, 1989. Nevertheless the unanimous adoption of even a watered-down proposal for UNDIL (Resolution 44/23) creates an opportunity which we can hope to utilize in the 1990s.

JUDGMENT OF LONDON NUCLEAR WARFARE TRIBUNAL

Tribunal members:

* Sean MacBride, Tribunal Chairman, winner of the 1974 Nobel Peace Prize and President of IPB;
* Richard Falk, Princeton Professor of International Law and Practice;
* Prof. Maurice Wilkins, who worked on the Manhattan Project in 1944 and in 1962 was awarded the Nobel Prize for Medicine;
* Prof. Dorothy Hodgkin OM, awarded the Nobel Prize for Chemistry in 1964.

The Tribunal heard witnesses and expert testimony over four days. Its full Judgment was only published in 1989, after MacBride's death. Some of its principal findings follow:

1. Any reliance on the threat or first use of nuclear weapons is a violation of international law, and constitutes a Crime against Humanity as set forth in the Nuremberg Principle 6(c).
2. Strategic doctrines and official war plans that contemplate first use or first strike with nuclear weapons constitute serious violations of international law, even if postures are only preparatory and contingent, and are never consummated in the form of an actual threat or use of nuclear weapons.
3. The development, production, and deployment of nuclear weapons systems with first-strike characteristics are aggravated instances of unlawful preparations...and constitute a violation of the Nuremberg prohibition on plans and conspiracies to wage aggressive war.
4. The use of nuclear weapons in a retaliatory mode, after prior armed attack and in accordance with the concept of self-defence in the United Nations Charter, is nevertheless unlawful unless such use is discriminate, proportionate, and without poisonous or unnecessarily cruel effects; since it seems impossible to satisfy such criteria, any use of nuclear weapons, whatever the pretext or justification, is an unlawful and criminal act of war entailing both governmental and individual responsibility.
5. As a consequence of (4), any form of deterrent threat to use nuclear weapons, even if limited to defensive and retaliatory situations, is a continuing violation of the laws of war; at a minimum, overcoming deterrence with all deliberate speed is an implicit legal duty for political and military leaders representing governments of nuclear weapons states. (22)

The eighties also saw the expansion of an international peace movement able to network more effectively across frontiers and to co-operate with increasingly assertive neutral governments and citizen groups known as non-governmental organisations or NGOs. Examples include:

* the *European Nuclear Disarmament* movement (END) which promoted cross-bloc solidarity and which has led to the *Helsinki Citizens Assembly* process, centred in Prague;
* the *Great Peace Journey* organised by the Swedish section of the Women's International League for Peace and Freedom (WILPF) to ask Foreign Ministries whether they would agree to various disarmament measures if all the other nations did the same. With a very few shameful exceptions, nearly all said they would!
* the *Greenham Common Women's Peace Camp* became an inspiration and a magnet for women from all over the world; when some Greenham Women Against Cruise sought an injunction against President Reagan they were helped by very many groups and experts, including the Centre for Constitutional Rights and two US Senators (25);
* the IPB's programme of educational work from 1981 to highlight the illegality and immorality of nuclear weapons, which has involved specialist international conferences and from 1987 a massive petition signed by 11,000 lawyers, of the very highest distinction;
* after the Gulf war the *International War Crimes Tribunal*, initiated by former US Attorney-General Ramsey Clark. In 20 countries and 24 US cities hearings were held at which evidence accumulated of the criminal anti-civilian thrust of much of the Allied bombing effort (26).

LAWYERS APPEAL AGAINST NUCLEAR WAR (MACBRIDE PETITION)

The late Sean MacBride was a politician, human rights lawyer and senior UN civil servant with a very distinguished international reputation. In 1987 as President of the IPB he launched a historic Lawyers Appeal which called for the prohibition of nuclear weapons and declared that

'the use, for whatever reason, of a nuclear weapon would constitute

a) a violation of international law

b) a violation of human rights, and

c) a crime against humanity'.

The petition, which also drew attention to the risks of accidental nuclear war and its ecological consequences, was launched in 1987 and is due to be presented to the Secretary-General of the Conference on Disarmament in Geneva in May 1992. It was signed by 11,000 lawyers from 56 countries, including:

* Justices T.O. Elias (Nigeria) and Mohammed Bedjaoui (Algeria), then Judges at the World Court in the Hague;
* Ministers of Justice, Attorney-Generals, Ombudsmen, Chief Justices, scores of senior judges, professors of law, legislators, senior counsel, presidents of national bar associations, etc;
* The chairmen of the Union of Arab Lawyers, the Union of South American Lawyers, and the Secretary-General of the Inter-African Union of Lawyers;
* The Secretary-General of the International Commission of Jurists and the President of the International Association of Democratic Lawyers.

The response to this appeal clearly shows the enormous potential contribution of the international legal profession in this field, which IALANA and the World Court Project will seek to build on systematically.

Note on Terminology

Every movement which is serious about its liberation has to question the language of the status quo - witness women's challenges to the use of selective terms like 'mankind' and 'he'. The present Guide frequently avoids terms such as 'nuclear weapons' 'bombs' or 'arms', preferring to talk of nuclear 'preparations', 'devices', 'strategies', etc. In other places I put quotation marks round these words and other terms such as nuclear 'retaliation', 'deterrence' and the 'nuclear first strike'/'second strike' distinction. (Quotations using 'bomb-speak' remain unchanged.)

In my view instruments of warfare should be named according to how they effect the majority of people. From our point of view as civilians, all nuclear 'weapons' are first poison. They are not like *bona fide* arms (The Latin root *arma* has a defensive meaning, as in 'armour'). Real weapons are very often used in an indiscriminate or terrorist way, but they can in principle also be used in a lawful, focused manner to defend a population against invading troops. By contrast the blast- and even fire-effects of nuclear pseudo-weapons are not the main effects. Many people downgrade the radiation-related consequences to a category of side-effects causing incidental collateral damage. But from a civilian point of view these latter effects are primary in terms of numbers affected by long-term damage to health and genetic systems. This kind of mass poisoning can't be targeted accurately; it doesn't fit into the two-actor scenario of nations 'hitting each other', like two boys fighting in a school playground.

It is time to abandon the male-defined military model of 'the Bomb' and name the machines in question accurately from our own perspective: as poison-scattering devices.

Keith Mothersson

3. The World Court Project... a story of growing support

March 1987: Harold Evans, a retired district judge from Christchurch, sends an Open Letter to the Prime Ministers of New Zealand and Australia asking them to initiate action which will lead to an advisory opinion 'on the legality (or otherwise) of nuclear weaponry at international law'. Evans reminds them of the occasion in 1973/4 when their two countries had taken France to the World Court over its atmospheric nuclear testing in the Pacific. He includes supporting statements from six distinguished legal specialists.

Australian Prime Minister Bob Hawke expresses sympathy but considers arms control negotiations a more promising avenue for disarmament (without apparently considering whether an advisory opinion might complement negotiations). Initially David Lange is cautiously encouraging but powerful elements in the NZ Foreign Ministry combine to block the Evans proposal despite unanimous endorsement in November 1988 of the government's own Advisory Committee on Peace and Disarmament. The proposal is formally rejected in September 1989.

Ambassador Richard Butler (Australia) and Brett Lineham (Head of Disarmament Section, Ministry of Foreign Affairs, NZ) at the UNSSOD III March, New York,

Peace activists in Aoteoroa/New Zealand and Australia are convinced that political and economic anxieties (over alienating the US and NATO members of the European Community) have triumphed over considerations of law. They continue to approach governments and citizens groups for support.

In 1987:

* Evans writes a lengthy Open Letter to all 71 UN Member States having diplomatic accreditation in Canberra and Wellington asking them to bring a UN resolution, perhaps collectively. Many diplomats express interest and forward the proposal to their governments.

* Support is elicited from the *NZ and Australian sections of the International Commission of Jurists*, who argue that seeing the Rule of Law as a dynamic concept means that they cannot ignore the nuclear threat to human rights.

1988:

* Evans addresses NZ section of *International Physicians for the Prevention of Nuclear War* (IPPNW) who subsequently win formal support for a reference from IPPNW at its Montreal Congress.

1989:

* The *International Peace Bureau* endorses this strategy at its annual conference held in Brighton, UK (Sept.89).

* At its First World Congress in October at the Hague the *International Association of Lawyers Against Nuclear Arms* (IALANA) pass resolutions appealing to all UN Member States to take steps to request an advisory opinion on Use. (ch. 18, Role of Lawyers) IALANA also adopts a Policy Plan including 'raising the question...in all the appropriate legal fora', mobilising professional bodies, and setting up a sub-committee.

* On his way home, Evans lobbies Commonwealth Heads of Government meeting in Kuala Lumpur, with help from Malaysian IPPNW.

Harold Evans with NZ Peace Activists Katie Boanas & Alyn Ware

1990:

* Lobbying of Commonwealth Bar Association meeting in Aotearoa in April.
* With practical help from grass roots trade unions, the UK-based *Institute for Law and Peace* (INLAP) produces 12pp briefing paper which circulates fairly widely in UK and abroad.
* Some lobbying of August Non-Proliferation Review Conference in Geneva, including informal meeting for diplomats jointly called by INLAP and IPB. Cautious interest from diplomats from Philippines, Mexico, Yugoslavia.
* 5th International Conference of *Nuclear-Free Zone Local Authorities*, held in Glasgow in November, includes in subsequent declaration references to criminality of nuclear preparations and resolves:

  '(c) to co-operate with IALANA, the IPB and other progressive NGOs and nations to secure a UN reference to the World Court and to lay the groundwork for this momentous request by amassing thousands of legally significant declarations.'

1991:

* January: interest expressed by Human Rights Advisor to President Havel of the Czech and Slovak Federative Republic.

* March: NZ peaceworker Alyn Ware approaches a number of diplomatic missions in New York, and finds considerable support among those prominent in the 'Group of 21' and guarded interest from some neutrals. Subsequently consultations between diplomats and their governments begin and tentative inter-diplomatic discussions on the scope of the resolution, co-sponsorship, and timing.

* Congress of IPPNW meeting in Stockholm in June resolves much more active support for the ICJ campaign and passes second resolution:

  ' that IPPNW...organise a campaign for the setting up of an international control agency to oversee the destruction of existing nuclear stockpiles' and to research the necessary practical steps.'

Subsequently, the New Zealand section of IPPNW, which has spearheaded the resolutions, produces a fine series of discussion papers, written by Erich Geiringer, and also begins active lobbying of WHO delegations in 1992.

* June/July: Kiwi Katie Boanas and IPB Secretary-General Colin Archer approach a number of Southern diplomatic missions in Geneva and receive considerable support for what is seen as a 'non-discriminatory' basis for progress in nuclear disarmament and non-proliferation.

* *Women's International League for Peace and Freedom* (WILPF) passes resolution at its July international conference held in Norway:

  ' urging international executive committee to join with other organisations...and...delegations of member states of the UN, in seeking moves in the UN General Assembly...to request an advisory opinion on the illegality or otherwise of nuclear weapons in international law'

* Visit to UK of Katie Boanas. A meeting called by INLAP which she addresses resolves to create a joint UK body to promote this strategy, to be known as *UK section of the World Court Project* (WCP);

* Standing Committee of the *World Peace Council* meeting in Brazzaville agrees to support WCP and to encourage their affiliates and contacts to become active;
* Fifth World Conference of *Friends World Committee for Consultation*, meeting in August in Kenya, receives a report recommending Quaker involvement in the ICJ-campaign, and commends this to Friends everywhere 'for study and action as they see fit';
* The 17th meeting of the influential Pacific Concerns Resource Centre, serving as the secretariat of the *Nuclear Free and Independent Pacific Movement*, held in Suva, Fiji in September 1991, declares its active support.
* On behalf of IALANA and New York-based *US Lawyers Committee on Nuclear Policy*, Prof. Saul Mendlovitz sounds out diplomatic opinion in New York.

1992:

* Second World Assembly of *IALANA* in January in Amsterdam commits itself to increased priority for ICJ-case promotion among the legal profession and diplomatic community. An additional meeting attended by delegates from 13 IALANA affiliates and 2 lay activists agrees to:

- unite provisionally behind promotion of a resolution on Use and Threat to use nuclear weapons;
- support the international launch and seminar for World Court Project in Geneva in May, jointly with IPPNW and main event organisers IPB;
- publish a short Memorandum for governments, diplomats, lawyers, and journalists outlining the basic case for the Advisory opinion;
- set up a diplomatic/political database (IALANA), and a citizens groups data base in Geneva (IPB) with a view to systematic lobbying and networking efforts;
- seek a popular dimension for the reference (and financial contributions) by inviting members of the public to sign declarations of the public conscience as practised by WCP-UK.
- IPPNW begins lobbying of delegations to the World Health Assembly. This results in a resolution from Colombia to the May WHA meeting (*see footnote at end of Chapter 10*)

A range of other groups at both national and international levels are currently believed to support at least an initial advisory request concerning Use (or Use and Threat). In a number of other influential bodies a lively debate has begun but formal support has not yet been achieved.

NUCLEARISM EQUALS NIHILISM

It represents the ultimate injustice, the ultimate violation of human rights and religious responsibilities, the ultimate environmental catastrophe. In short it represents the the ultimate negation of every human value which women and men, and children too, have ever lived and died for and struggled and argued and studied and worked to secure.

In promoting the World Court Project in the Decade of International Law as a potentially unifying focus for NGOs and non-nuclear nations we do not seek to compete with other concerns.

Rather we are conscious that we stand on the shoulders of Henri Dunant and generations of unsung heroes and heroines in many movements and countries - in order to at least put this most terrible menace behind us, and thereby contribute to securing the values they all struggled to realize.

We also propose co-operation in the belief that the World Court reference strategy can help to accustom certain nations to not having an automatic right to control and veto all new developments. By weakening their confidence and strengthening the side of the global anti-nuclear majority, we suggest that the World Court Project can incidentally serve many causes by paving the way for more general and far-reaching reform of the UN system itself (26).

Part Two: A Guide to International Law

Opening session at the International Court of Justice, the principal judicial organ of the UN

UN photo VW/gf

The 1989 session of the Conference on Disarmament began on 7 February at the United Nations Office at Geneva. This is a general view of the opening meeting which was presided over by Aldo Pugliese (Italy).

UN photo 173,163

4. International Law - a short introduction

Comparison of national and international legal systems

National legal systems have:

A) a central **law-making** body;

B) a unified system of **law-enforcement** - police, courts, jails, and so on;

C) a way of resolving disputes by reference to common standards authoritatively declared. (1)

A) Law-making:

By comparison, the international legal system lacks a unified World Parliament. But many jurists would say that when it passes unanimous resolutions the General Assembly moves from 'talking shop' to virtual legislature. The same applies in cases of quasi-unanimity (over 90%) so long as every kind of legal system is represented in the majority. (2)

International legislation comes about mainly through an ad hoc patchwork process of treaties and conventions which nations may or may not sign and then ratify, with or without reservations (which the other signatories may or may not accept). This is quite unlike national law - also confusingly called *'domestic'* or *'municipal'* law. Individual citizens do not have the choice as to whether or not to be bound for instance by a law against driving when drunk, and if so, whether to enter a declaration reserving their right to do so.

However proceeding by consent is arguably preferable and it can be a source of strength, since the individual nations will be more committed to helping implement the treaties which they make or subsequently accede to (3).

B) Law-enforcement:

There is no veto-free world police force or unified criminal justice system. The Security Council has primary responsibility for enforcing all laws whose breach results or could result in a threat to world security (Chapter VII of the Charter). It can decree provisional measures to stop conflicts worsening, e.g. deploy peace-keeping troops. It can make generally binding rules, e.g. imposing sanctions or a compulsory anti-nuclear regime for Iraq. It can also act as an armed international police force - but only through a Military Staff Committee of military chiefs of its five permanent members. Any other arrangement is quite unconstitutional, as was the pseudo-UN force in the Gulf war.

THE RELEVANCE OF INTERNATIONAL LAW

We are aware of public scepticism. Many citizens and officials continue to query whether international law is really law in the absence of police mechanisms for enforcement... Our response here is that international law provides the underpinning for many varieties of transnational life that work so well we take it for granted. An effective legal order does not necessarily depend on central institutions for decision and enforcement. Law can be effective if the parties seek to make it so out of reasons of convenience, mutual benefit, a sense of right and respect, or even because they find value in a reputation of law-abidingness....

Of course, all law is violated at times. Indeed, enforcement would be superfluous were compliance perfect. The special problem of international life arises because some violations are so totally disruptive and unacceptable in their effects. It is important to be clear that preventing a particular kind of violation is a different challenge to a legal order than a denial of its existence altogether.

- from Para 1.1 of the *Judgment of the London Nuclear Warfare Tribunal* (4)

The lack of a unified world police force and international criminal court is not necessarily a source of weakness in the global legal system. Sometimes norms can best be enforced on a polycentric basis, witness the vigilance of neighbours co-operating to keep hard-drugs dealers out of a locality. In any case:

'The question is not whether international law is enforced but whether it is in fact observed...In the words of a leading modern writer, it is probably true that 'almost all nations observe almost all the principles of international law and almost all of their obligations almost all of the time'.' (5)

For many offences a universal jurisdiction already exists, e.g. piracy. This means that any state anywhere can put on trial people suspected of piracy, no matter what their nationality or where their crimes took place; if not they ought to extradite on request. 'No hiding place' has also been decreed for war criminals (following Nuremberg), and increasingly, through extradition provisions attached to multilateral conventions, for aeroplane hijackers, major drug-dealers and terrorists. If a unified system of criminal justice ever came into being, it would inherit this ever-thickening web of inter-jurisdictional co-operation.

Another example concerns genocide. In ratifying the 1948 *UN Convention on the Prevention and Punishment of the Crime of Genocide* states have theoretically lost the freedom of decision whether or not to move against those suspected of conspiracy to genocide and are bound to 'enact...the necessary legislation to give effect to the provisions of the present Convention'.

AN INTERNATIONAL CRIMINAL COURT?

Numerous proposals have also been put forward - including by Sean MacBride - for an international criminal court. With an impartial composition, its findings would avoid the suspicion of victors' justice which hung over the post-WW2 war-crimes trials.

Another major benefit would be that states could provide the court with prima facie evidence of serious crime, and if the alleged perpetrator was at large and declined to come forward to clear his name, a trial could proceed using defence counsel appointed by the court. (In this way Noriega could have been declared a world outlaw without hundreds of civilians being killed and the virtual annexation of Panama by the US.)

At the request of the General Assembly in 1981 the International Law Commission has resumed work (suspended in 1954 for want of a definition of aggression) on a *Draft Code of Offences Against the Peace and Security of Mankind*, for an international criminal court to implement. One reason for progress being so slow is the work involved in considering different legal systems and their codes. Another is the political sensitivity of the issue - in the above example, Noriega could perhaps have counter-indicted Bush! (6)

Recommendations will also be considered concerning the procedural machinery and ways to insulate decision-making from political pressures. This is important because there could be dangers in proceeding if there was a risk of a single powerful nation capturing and abusing the machinery for its own ends.

C) Dispute Resolution:

Another vital condition for any legal system is some authoritative procedure for resolving disputes by reference to common standards. For countries wanting to settle disputes peacefully, there are ample possibilities for conciliation, mediation, and referring the dispute jointly to the World Court or for arbitration. The problems arise when one party doesn't want a dispute to be arbitrated or judged. It may not be possible for the other party to prove the necessary jurisdiction for a court or tribunal to look into the merits of their complaint.

To that extent the rule of law is still patchy in international society and very much a reflection of current international relations. These relations can also include geo-political constraints, economic pressures, diplomatic clout, ideological penetration, covert operations and so on (7). A small country might have a well-founded grievance against a big one yet feel inhibited from taking it to the ICJ or the Human Rights Commission, for fear of unpleasant repercussions.

Increasing restraints on state sovereignty

The classic 'State Sovereignty' theory of international law (*Jus Gentium*) evolved in pre-democratic times when sovereigns were absolute rulers. Externally sovereigns could also do what they pleased unless it was forbidden:

* either by the terms of a voluntary *Treaty*, to specific clauses of which they could in any case make reservations and from which they could withdraw after giving notice as prescribed in the treaty;
* or by *Customary Rules* and principles.

Customary rules involve both facts and accompanying meanings and include widely observed customs and general principles (or State Practice), e.g. respecting each others' envoys, if only out of prudent self-interest. These rules and principles have to be 'generally' (NB not unanimously) recognised as being observed as a matter of legal obligation (referred to as *Opinio Juris*).

A degree of consent expressed through treaties or acceptance of a customary rule is still the normal basis of international law. But an increasing number of qualifications are creeping into the equation, which judges and other nations can use to restrain a state's freedom of action.

The extreme extension of the State Sovereignty position vacates all content from international law: by flouting or disagreeing with a rule (or 'derogating' from a treaty provision), it is claimed that any single nation can destroy its 'general acceptability', hence its status as a binding rule. Talk of international law then becomes a mere front, a useful whistle which big countries can blow against small ones as a pretext for the next (illegal) reprisal or intervention, rarely a net small nations can use to restrain big ones.

Jus gentium originally meant 'law of peoples or tribes' before it meant 'law of nations'. The law between peoples was conceived as an outgrowth based on settled customs within each of their societies. By the 18th and 19th centuries the law of nations was being reduced to mean the law between States. If States chose to wage war whenever the opportunity arose, this was no longer breach of the common code within countries encouraging peaceable relations - and besides, who was to stop them? Even where national courts were beginning to exercise a degree of control over what the rulers were doing internally, special legal doctrines were created to exempt the institutionalized double-standards of the rulers towards foreign Princes - and especially 'Infidel Moors' and supposed 'lesser breeds' seen as outside the scope of law and civilisation, who could be bullied and swindled with impunity.

These doctrines of 'act of state', 'raison d'Etat', 'executive privilege' still linger powerfully in many domestic legal systems, especially where war and national security are concerned. States seek to exclude from the jurisdiction of the International Court of Justice matters to do with their *'national security and vital interests'*. But such special pleading may not always cut much ice, as witness the *Nuremberg Principles*:

> 'II. *The fact that internal law does not impose a penalty for an act which constitutes a crime under international law does not relieve the person who committed it from responsibility under international law.*
>
> *III: The fact that a person who committed an act which constitutes a crime under international law acted as Head of State or responsible government official does not relieve him from responsibility.'*

Nor may any state run counter to a rule which the international community regards as especially *'necessary to protect the public interests of the society of States or to maintain the public morality recognized by them'* (8). Thus a new category of international law, called *jus cogens*, has been recognised **from which no nation may derogate**, just as the public interest within a nation would not allow a man recklessly pursuing a quarrel over a garden fence to enter a reservation excluding himself from the operation of the laws against burning down his neighbour's house (and half the neighbourhood). If one of these especially weighty *peremptory norms* is found in a treaty, every nation is taken to have signed up for that section, and reservations are null and void. (9)

Although the category of *jus cogens* was officially recognised in Art. 53 of the 1969 *Vienna Convention on the Interpretation of Treaties* (10), no definitive list exists of which rules qualify for inclusion. Nearly all lawyers would include Non-aggression, Suppression of Piracy, Slavery and Genocide. Many would add Suppression of Grave War Crimes and Terrorism. Most describe Non-Destruction of the Common Environment as an 'emergent' norm in this *jus cogens* category.

With the development of state concern, state practice and public morality, rules which were formerly binding only as between parties to a treaty can become customary norms binding even on nations that have not signified their acceptance. The *Nuremberg Tribunal* held this to have happened between 1907 and 1939 in the case of the *Hague Conventions* (11). If treaties can subsequently give rise to customary rules, the reverse also occurs, indeed more commonly. Moral principles and State practices can come together first as recognised customary rules and then in due course diplomatic conferences explicitly formulate them in writing as the 'declaratory' provisions of a treaty.

The *UN Charter* reaffirmed the importance of the sovereign independence of each state - a valuable principle jealously guarded by new nations subjected to colonial (and now post-colonial) domination. But the Charter spells out a number of other fundamental principles which the kings of 18th century Europe would have seen as gross restrictions on their sovereignty and as interference in their internal affairs. More and more questions are gradually being removed from the sole exclusive jurisdiction of States. Legally, they are no longer free to engage in genocide and grave human rights abuses, to attack their neighbours or otherwise menace international security, e.g. by attempting to acquire biological or nuclear 'weapons'. In principle, the Security Council could recommend or take action against all such nations - though this consistent approach is not being followed in practice.

Less is now heard about the rights of states, more about their duties:

* to their citizenry and sub-national groups;
* to assist the UN and to co-operate with each other according to the UN Charter and the important Declaration on Friendly Relations of 1970 (12);
* to be good neighbours and to avoid causing each other environmental harm, in accordance with the Stockholm Declaration of 1972;
* to respect parts of the planet which do not belong to any nation and which should be protected as part of the 'common heritage of Mankind', e.g. 1982 *Convention on the Law of the Sea.*

Increasingly, too, unrepresented peoples without statehood and non-governmental organisations are seeking to find a place in the international order bigger than their current toe-hold in consultative status with the *Economic and Social Council.* All these developments are modifying the classical picture of the near-absolute legal sovereignty of States, whose poisonous expression is the purported 'right' of the nuclear powers to defend themselves as they alone see fit in defiance of other nations and world civil society.

5. The International Court of Justice (ICJ)

Defined as 'the principal judicial organ' of the UN (Art.92 of Charter = C.92), the ICJ is the successor to the old League of Nations Court, the Permanent Court of International Justice (PCIJ). It has its seat at the Hague in the Palace of Peace, which also houses the Permanent Court of International Arbitration (PCIA), a vast legal library and the Hague Academy of International Law. Every year its proceedings and judgments are published in its *ICJ Reports*, *ICJ Pleadings* and *Yearbook*.

The Court is composed of 15 full-time judges who take an oath to serve impartially and conscientiously. Their salaries, pensions and diplomatic immunity are guaranteed by the UN and a judge can only be removed by a unanimous vote of the others. Through its founding Statute (13) appended to the UN Charter it has considerable autonomy:

* although based in the Netherlands, it can decide to hold hearings elsewhere (Statute Art.22 = S.22);
* it can make interim injunctions pending a final decision in contentious cases (S.41);
* it can 'entrust any individual ...or... organisation that it may select, with the task of carrying out an inquiry or giving an expert opinion' (S.50).
* it appoints its own officials and makes its own Rules (14).

Two kinds of jurisdiction

Since 1946 the Court has had 88 cases to deal with. These fell into two distinct categories: 68 were contentious cases, and 20 were advisory rulings given in response to requests by other UN bodies. Recent years have seen greater willingness by States to entrust their disputes to the ICJ (15).

In **contentious cases** the Court first has to establish the basis for it to assume jurisdiction over the dispute. If both parties make a joint approach to the Court, the Court can move straight onto the merits of the case. Often, however, one party tries to wriggle out of having to submit to the jurisdiction of the Court. In these cases the Court will survey a wide range of treaties to see whether the nation in question has at any time indicated its general consent to accept the jurisdiction of the Court in this kind of dispute.

Thus the question of who can take whom to the World Court is often extremely complicated. Each State has an obvious interest in not giving other States legal handles with which to be dragged to Court against its current will. But the reciprocity rule cuts both ways. If State A is unwilling to give any handles to State B to take it to Court, then if A ever wants to take B to Court, B will probably be able to evade jurisdiction by reversing A's restrictive conditions against it. Unfortunately a 'minimum world public order' (16) often appears to be an attractive option for big and powerful countries with other means of bending state B to their will!

Advisory jurisdiction

1. The General Assembly or the Security Council may request the ICJ to give an advisory opinion on any legal question.
2. Other organs of the United Nations and specialized agencies, which may at any time be so authorized by the GA, may also request advisory opinions of the Court on legal questions arising within the scope of their activities.' (C.96)

In the 1950 advisory case known as *Interpretation of Peace Treaties*, the Court distinguished the two kinds of cases thus:

> '*The consent of States, parties to a dispute, is the basis of the Court's jurisdiction in contentious cases. The situation is different in regard to advisory proceedings even where the Request for an Opinion relates to a legal question actually pending between States. The Court's reply is only of an advisory character; as such, it has no binding force. It follows that no State...can prevent the giving of an Advisory* ***Opinion which the United Nations considers to be desirable in order to obtain enlightenment as to the course of action it should take. The Court's opinion is not given to the States, but to the organ which is entitled to request it;*** *the reply of the Court, itself an 'organ of the United Nations', represents its participation in the activities of the organization, and, in principle, should not be refused.*' (17)

The Court has a particularly wide discretion in how it deals with advisory requests. However a procedure is laid down for the Court to invite all States and relevant international bodies to furnish written and oral statements and arguments and to receive and respond to each other's submissions.(S.67)

Sources of law to be applied

'The Court, whose function is to decide in accordance with international law such disputes as are submitted to it, shall apply:

(a) international conventions, whether general or particular, establishing rules expressly recognized by the contesting States;

(b) international custom, as evidence of a general practice accepted as law;

(c) the general principles of law recognized by civilised nations;

(d) judicial decisions and the teachings of the most highly qualified publicists of the various nations, as subsidiary means for the determination of rules of law.' (S.38.1)

Although extremely authoritative, this listing is not exhaustive. Other 'subsidiary means' which the Court might use in order to establish the existence (or otherwise) of a rule of law, include

* decisions of international organisations, including unanimous (or otherwise) resolutions of UN bodies;
* diplomatic correspondence, protest notes (or their absence) and the proceedings of diplomatic conferences leading to the conclusion or non-conclusion of treaties;
* national laws and regulations (e.g. the Nuremberg Tribunal took German military manuals into account), policy statements, press conferences and the opinions of government legal advisers;
* especially so far as the law of war is concerned, non-governmental pronouncements which throw light on the 'public conscience' (ch. 13).

Approach of the court

The PCIJ and initially the ICJ followed the classical Western school of jurisprudence, which has been called 'judicial positivism' (18). This was characterised by the following traits:

* primary emphasis on the sovereignty of states;
* concentration on the exact terms of treaties seen as being like formal contracts;
* 'judicial self-restraint', e.g. reluctance to intervene in 'political' affairs, seen as a distinct domain;
* thinking of the law as 'science' and denying both the values involved in adopting this approach and the political repercussions;
* preoccupation with technical and procedural questions, thus implicitly endorsing the status quo in the interests of the 'have' nations.

With increasing representation of the South the Court has gradually evolved a less conservative model of its role. It has dropped the insupportable notion of 'law' and 'politics' in two watertight compartments. The new 'judicial politic' of cautious intervention (19) means:

* greater readiness to grasp substantive nettles, rather than to hide behind procedural technicalities;
* greater emphasis on the law being widely respected as just, rather than merely clear and predictable;
* willingness by small steps to assist in the development (not just restatement) of international law, if the Court feels that it can thereby contribute to the evolution of global public policy and the resolution of problems in the international community.

Accordingly the judges may be inclined or bound to interpret treaties and customary rules in the light of:

* what the original context and aims of these provisions were;
* what honouring this spirit would mean today in the light of the evolution of the modern world;
* what 'soft law' declarations may have been made which may point to the emergence of a new rule of customary international law (eg UN resolutions and other condemnations of Apartheid, *Nicaragua* 1971)

Justiciability

However the Court remains acutely aware of the geo-political context within which it operates, and that if excessive reliance is placed on the legal avenue for resolving disputes, this could be counter-productive in the absence of an emerging diplomatic consensus or quasi-consensus (20). This occurred when a Cold War dispute about the role of UN troops in the Congo was referred to the ICJ by a General Assembly vote of 52-11 with 32 abstentions. Western efforts to use the resulting Opinion to force the minority to pay for UN actions the minority opposed, on pain of expulsion from the UN, had to be dropped as counter-productive. (21)

If, rightly or wrongly, the Court feels it is being asked to make too great a leap, it may opt to evade the core of an issue (see Box) or decline jurisdiction altogether on the grounds that the issue is 'unripe for judicial settlement' (22).

NUCLEAR TESTS CASE

In May 1973 Australia and New Zealand took France to the ICJ in connection with its plans to continue atmospheric nuclear 'tests' (poison-spreading) in the South Pacific. France argued that the Court lacked jurisdiction and refused to appear or file pleadings once the Court issued orders insisting that France cease its testing pending the resolution of the case. France tested twice more. Then it announced that it had finished that phase of its research, and would only need to test underground. The Court majority seized on this to evade ruling on whether it had jurisdiction, let alone on the substance of the case. It read into France's bald, almost defiant, announcement a legally-self-binding commitment not to test in the atmosphere.

Such an extension of the law concerning state declarations and their ability to create legally binding obligations - even without any reference to legal considerations in the text of the announcement - put the Court on the side of the anti-nuclear angels. But it then removed the case from its roster on the grounds that the dispute 'no longer had any object'. But as the joint dissenting opinion pointed out, Australia had not just asked for the tests to be stopped. Its main aim had been a declaratory judgment that causing nuclear pollution to other countries was unlawful, and New Zealand had **only** asked the Court for this. Hopefully the Court has become bolder since.

Nevertheless, especially in an Advisory Opinion, the Court would usually feel responsible to assist the UN sister-body asking for the opinion and thereby help the world community resolve the substantive issues at stake.

> *'Law cannot be 'neutral' or 'objective' with respect to contending interpretations of history and opposed positions of interest in the global system. Above all, the Court is uniquely qualified to offer, in its advisory capacity especially, an arena for discussing and perhaps even resolving normative controversy. This opportunity exists particularly in big cases, where the legal form of the controversy sets the stage for an educative jurisprudence.'* (23)

The Court is not strictly speaking bound by its previous findings (S.59). But it is bound to give the reasons for its decisions (S.56) and it is aware that its reputation depends on evolving a reasonably stable approach. Hence we can review certain principles already enunciated which might bear on the justiciability of the nuclear issue, i.e. the readiness of the Court to grasp this 'hot potato':

* Are factual questions unsuitable for the court? No. 'A mixed question of law and fact is none the less a legal question' within the meaning of Art.96 of the Charter (24). The Court considers itself as competent as anyone else to investigate and interpret even very complicated facts (25).

* On the other hand 'the Court may give an advisory opinion on **any** legal question, abstract or otherwise' [emphasis added] since it presumes its views are sought 'for a practical and contemporary purpose' (26)

* Is there an inherent problem if an issue is also being dealt with in some other forum? In *Aegean Sea Continental Shelf* (Greece v Turkey), the Court disposed of this objection, noting that 'Negotiation and judicial settlement are enumerated together in Article 33 of the Charter of the UN as means for the peaceful settlement of disputes'. The Court considers that its legal findings can **contribute to a process** which may well also involve bilateral negotiations and the various parts of the UN machinery working in a complementary fashion (27).

* Are there some issues which the Security Council is entitled to

monopolize? When the US used this argument in the *Nicaragua* case, having been shielded by the British use of the veto in the Security Council, the Court rejected this argument (28). Of course the UN Charter provides:

While the Security Council [SC] is exercising in respect of any dispute or situation the functions assigned to it in the present Charter, the General Assembly [GA] shall not make any recommendation...unless the Security Council so requests.' (C.12.1)

But this does not apply to the ICJ. (29)

How judges are elected

Judges are elected for nine-year terms, but may be re-elected. New appointees are jointly elected by simple majorities in both the General Assembly and the Security Council (NB. no veto for permanent members) - or by the other judges if the General Assembly and Security Council remain deadlocked after various reserve decision-procedures have been exhausted. (Arts. 11 and 12)

A) Global representativeness

In voting for candidates nations should bear in mind

'that in the body [of the Court] as a whole the representation of the main forms of civilization and of the principal legal systems of the world should be assured.' (Art.9)

Whereas the old League of Nations Court was very heavily European/ white-dominated, the current ICJ has a more representative composition, which is vital to ensuring its legitimacy. Nevertheless a declining degree of 'Eurocentrism' still remains, partly through the general dominance of America and the 'West' in the legal profession (as in other spheres), and partly through residual over-representation on the Court.

The present distribution is Western Europe 4 members out of 15, Eastern Europe 2, North America 1, Sub-Saharan Africa 2 (one Francophone, civil law code; one Anglophone, common law), Arabs only 1, 'Latin' America and Caribbean only 2, and all of Asia only 3 seats (with over half the world's population). Elections to the ICJ are being fought with increasing intensity, so it is quite likely that this informal carve-up could be challenged in the fall of 1993, when the next elections are due, e.g. with Non-Aligned countries voting for replacement candidates from China and Japan and Africa, and one other Asian country and one from a South American or Arab country, thus squeezing out one or two European candidates.

'Reprisals are themselves violations...the very nature of modern weapons are such that nuclear weapons should never be allowed to be used, never as first use, never as reprisals...The use of nuclear weapons is the ultimate crime... We can formulate all kinds of scenarios but that doesn't change the basic approach that there are certain weapons of warfare that are illegal and criminal and the behaviour of the other party doesn't make them legal....One thing quite clear to me is that according to the UN Charter we have an obligation to get rid of all nuclear weapons.'

Judge Jens Evensen, the first ever judge to be elected without a dissenting vote in either the Security Council or the General Assembly, speaking at a UN press conference at the Hague, April 1989.

B) Personal qualities

Within each legal-cultural/geographic region, voting nations are meant to vote without heed to nationality:

> *'The Court shall be composed of a body of independent judges, elected regardless of their nationality from among persons of high moral character, who possess the qualifications required in their respective countries for appointment to the highest judicial offices, or are jurisconsults [legal consultants, KM] of recognized competence in international law.'*

Judges are not supposed to represent their countries' political lines, but to serve impartially and with full independence. Member governments are paying increasingly detailed attention to the known views and record of candidates.

Ideal nominees will have:

* practical experience as a judge
* academic experience/reputation, including participation in the International Law Institute,etc and perhaps the UN's 34-member International Law Commission
* service as consultant to one or more governments
* experience as legal advisor to national delegations at key conferences and at the UN where they will have participated in the Sixth (legal) committee of the General Assembly
* been nominated by several national groups from different Regions.

* All this without being susceptible to blackmail by the secret services of certain nuclear nations!

For some reason being a man seems hitherto to have been a vital qualification. Hopefully, growing awareness of institutional sexism may perhaps make being a woman an advantage in future elections - although of course this, by itself, is no guarantee of legal soundness on the nuclear question.

C) Nominations

These are handled by the Secretary General who asks the official nominators of each country to nominate up to four persons, no more than two of their own nationality. Before a national group of nominators reports back to the Secretary General (not their Foreign Ministries) it is:

> *recommended to consult its highest court of justice, its legal faculties and schools of law, and its national academies and national sections of international academies devoted to the study of law.' (Art.6)*

Nominating groups are committees of four or fewer jurists who have either been specially chosen by their Foreign Ministries for this purpose or have been previously enrolled for the panel of arbitrators available to serve on the (largely inactive) Permanent Court of International Arbitration.

At all events there is scope for reform-minded jurists to check that the nominating machinery of their country is in place, and not just running on administrative inertia but rather is responsive to progressive currents of jurisprudence.

(See following page for current composition)

CURRENT COMPOSITION

Robert Jennings (President) [UK] term expires 2000 AD
(Presidential term expires after three years, unless re-elected)

Manfred Lachs [Poland] 1994
Shigeru Oda [Japan] 1994
Ni Zhengyu [China] 1994
Jens Evensen [Norway] 1994
Bola Ajibola [Nigeria] 1994

Mohammed Bedjaoui [Algeria] 1997
Roberto Ago [Italy] 1997
Stephen Schwebel [USA]
Nikolai Tassarov [CIS] 1997
Mohammed Shahabuddeen [Guyana] 1997

Andres Aguilar [Venezuela] 2000
Gilbert Guillaume [France] 2000
Raymond Ranjeva [Madagascar] 2000
Christopher Weeramantry [Sri Lanka] 2000

6. General limits to force and military necessity

The UN Charter expresses

* the **determination** 'to save succeeding generations from the scourge of war'
* the **objective** 'that force shall not be used, save in the common interest' (1st and 7th preambular points)
* the organisational **purpose** 'to maintain international peace and security' (Article 1) and
* the binding **principles** that Members

2 (3) shall settle their disputes peacefully without endangering international security and justice, and

2 (4) 'shall refrain...from the threat or use of force against the territorial integrity or political independence of any State, or in any other manner inconsistent with the Purposes of the UN'.

However nations are permitted one exception to this basic 'No Force' rule:

> *'Nothing in the present Charter shall impair the inherent right of individual or collective self-defence if an armed attack occurs against a Member of the UN, until the Security Council has taken measures necessary to maintain international peace and security.'*

Although this Article 51 has been the subject of much dispute, Nagendra Singh (30), Ian Brownlie (31) and other distinguished jurists have surely been right to argue that the inherent or customary right of self-defence was from 1945 onwards modified (so far as UN Member States are concerned) by being hedged about with two specific treaty requirements. Force may only be used **after an armed attack** and only **until the Security Council takes the necessary action.**

Although the customary right of self-defence includes the right to go to the defence of other nations, the traditional formulation of this general right is otherwise very restrictive (32). Even when the legitimacy of 'anticipatory self-defence' has been conceded in principle, it is required to match up to the Caroline criteria. In 1837 Britain made an armed intervention across the Canadian border against an American ship, the US Secretary of State, Webster, demanded that Britain:

> *'show a necessity of self-defence, instant, overwhelming, leaving no choice of means and no moment for deliberation'. (Even if Britain was justified by these tests, it should also show that its local commanders) 'did nothing unreasonable or excessive, since the act, justified by the necessity of self-defence, must be limited by that necessity and kept clearly within it'* (33).

The degree of force used should not be disproportionate to the degree of danger threatened, eg a border skirmish is no excuse for taking over a country. On signing the 1928 Pact of Paris renouncing war of aggression, the US made a reservation that 'it alone is competent to decide whether circumstances require recourse to war in self-defence'. When Nazi Germany claimed to be acting in self-defence, the Nuremberg Tribunal rejected its claim to be the sole judge of the degree of national peril it was allegedly responding to with each fresh invasion.

> *'Whether action taken under the claimed right of self-defence was in fact aggressive or defensive must ultimately be subject to investigation and adjudication if international law is ever to be enforced.'* (34)

The UN Charter builds on the Pact of Paris by requiring countries using force in self-defence to report their action and their reasons to the Security Council - which can check claims and could order it to stop.

Hague Convention IV of 1907 lays down a fundamental rule which is now binding on all governments and in respect of war by air and sea as well as land:

> ***'The right of belligerents to adopt means of injuring the enemy is not unlimited.'*** *(Regulation 22)*

This applies to 'holy wars', defensive wars, all wars - and even to reprisal actions as we shall see. No matter which side is in the right so far as the law governing resort to force is concerned (*jus ad bellum*), neither side may overthrow the rules governing the conduct of hostilities (*jus in bello*).

Limits to military necessity

These rules are the product of the interaction of certain principles. On the one side of the balance we can envisage *Military Necessity* (35). Unless counterbalanced by other factors this will justify anything which brings about the submission of the enemy as quickly as possible and with as few casualties as possible. Since the Pact of Paris (if not earlier) military necessity is not supposed to be invoked to justify uses of force which go beyond the aim of making the enemy retreat and forcing 'him' to come to just terms. Force used for total annihilation or in pursuit of a secret political agenda of post-war control or territorial expansion could not be said to be militarily necessary.

On the other side of the scales sit the *Principles of Humanity and Chivalry* (36). *Chivalry* rules out:

* a sneak attack not preceded by a declaration of hostilities;
* waging a 'war of no quarter', ie without permitting the enemy to surrender;
* the killing and humiliation of prisoners of war;
* dishonest tricks with enemy uniforms, white flags and the sign of the Red Cross or Crescent.

The principle of *Humanity* insists that the term 'defence' should really mean what it says and not be permitted to provide a blanket excuse for the murder of harmless people unconnected with the war effort and even pointless cruelty to enemy combatants.

A good example of the tussle between 'the necessities of war' and the 'requirements of humanity' comes from the *Declaration of St Petersburg* of 1868, which outlawed projectiles weighing **less than** 400 grammes containing explosive or inflammable substances on the grounds that men soldiers would in any case be put out of action if hit by ordinary bullets. The extremely authoritative Preamble reads:

> *'Considering...that the only legitimate object which States should endeavour to accomplish during war is to weaken the* ***military*** *forces of the enemy;*
>
> *That for this purpose it is sufficient to disable the greatest possible number of men;*
>
> *That this object would be exceeded by the employment of* ***arms which uselessly aggravate the sufferings of disabled men, or render their death inevitable;***
>
> *That the employment of such arms would, therefore, be contrary to the laws of humanity.'* (emphasis added)

Neither side of the equation is static: although military measures and counter-measures evolve so too do people's conceptions of what is uncivilised, inhumane and 'excessive', often referred to as 'the laws of humanity and the dictates of the public conscience' (Martens clause, see below). Although World War Two showed that public opinion in Britain and the US could be manipulated to 'justify' fire-storms in the cities of a virtually defeated nation, a more reliable gauge of the standard of civilised behaviour derives from the reaction of neutral countries.

Changes in technology likewise cut two ways. At the beginning of World War Two Britain came to realize that 'precision bombing' of arms factories in Germany was a fantasy. If the attempt were made by day, the planes would be shot down en route; if bombers flew really low over the target so as to minimize casualties to surrounding dwellings, the chances of being shot down by anti-aircraft fire greatly increased. Allied bombing chiefs then authorised night bombing from a high altitude which made accuracy impossible. The ideal of pinpoint bombing was quietly dropped to permit the saturation bombing of a whole area in which one or more legitimate military targets were known to be situated (37). Hence the Hamburg firestorm of July 1943 in which around 40,000 civilians were sacrificed on the altar of 'military necessity'.

By the time of the Dresden raid of Feb 13/14th, 1945, in which 70-130,000 died (38), accuracy had greatly improved and the Allies had complete command of the skies. They could easily have flown low to destroy the railway bridge which provided the main official justification for the raid (and which, being lightly hit was quickly repaired to permit Germany to reinforce her collapsing Eastern front). Close investigation of the bombing of Hiroshima and Nagasaki also discredits the claim of military necessity (39).

The atomic era then saw attempts made to rationalise threatening the most immense 'collateral damage' to civilians by reference to the 'absolute necessity' of hitting Soviet military industrial complex and command centres. At this point one of the main apologists of area bombing, the Air Ministry legal adviser, J.M.Spaight, sought to extricate himself from this immoral sliding scale:

> *'[In target-area bombing] the area included in the assault is not out of proportion to that which the actual objectives occupy. In atom bombing the disproportion is immense....one might say that target-area bombing remains anchored - under strain - to the rule of the military objective, which must now be regarded as international law; atom bombing breaks adrift.'* (40)

Especially in the 1970s and 80s attempts have been made to present non-strategic scenarios for the 'limited' 'war-fighting' use of nuclear weapons allegedly in conformity to the requirements of international law concerning Discrimination, Proportionality, Humanity, Superfluous Suffering, etc (41). According to this view smaller nuclear devices (down to 1 kiloton or less) can now be targeted with increasing accuracy on relatively isolated military targets at some distance from centres of population. But changes in military technology can also be read the other way. Developments in the manufacture and accurate delivery of conventional TNT-based warheads will usually mean that there is no military necessity to 'go nuclear' even to destroy a difficult 'high-value' military target such as an aircraft carrier on the high seas (42), or tanks dug into desert emplacements. When the enemy is a probably less well-armed non-nuclear country such as Iraq, military alternatives will certainly exist (and diplomatic ones too). When the enemy is a nuclear nation, crossing the nuclear threshold will very probably magnetise nuclear attack. As the eminent international jurist, Ian Brownlie, has protested:

> *'It is rather ridiculous to allow refined examples of putatively lawful use to dominate the legal regime [thus ignoring] the general context of conflict and the risk of escalation.'* (43)

Although claims of military necessity may be invoked to justify excessive slaughter, this is not a reason for bypassing the laws of war in favour of a purely moral appeal. This area of law is itself an arena where morality (the principle of Humanity) can get to grips with military necessity, as in the section of the 1907 *Hague Convention IV Regulations* concerned with Means of Injuring the Enemy. On some issues military necessity comes out uppermost:

> *'[it is especially forbidden] to destroy...the enemy's property,* ***unless such destruction is imperatively demanded by the necessities of war'*** *(Art.23g)*
>
> *'...all necessary steps must be taken to spare,* ***as far as possible,*** *buildings dedicated to religion, art, science or charitable purposes, historic monuments, hospitals...' (Art.27)*

But conversely, where no such vague phrases appear as possible 'get-outs' for military hawks, the other Hague Regulations must be considered to lay down **categorical rules to be followed irrespective of 'military necessity'** (44):

> *'[it is especially forbidden:]*
>
> *23 a) To employ poison or poisoned weapons;...*
>
> *e) To employ arms, projectiles, or material calculated [French 'apt'] to cause unnecessary suffering;'*

These and other rules cannot be swept aside by the military whenever military expediency prompts as four of the current nuclear powers were subsequently to insist in the post-war trials of major war criminals. In 1947 a US Military Tribunal declared:

> *'it is of the essence of war that one or the other side must lose and the experienced generals or statesmen knew this when they drafted the rules and customs of land warfare [which are] designed specifically for all phases of war.'* (45)

The following year a British Tribunal ruled that

> *'military necessity or expediency do not justify a violation of positive rules....The rules of international law must be followed even if it results in the loss of a battle or even a war.'* (46)

Provided that their opponent is taking prisoners, nobody is forced to violate the laws of war in extreme circumstances. So far as 'self-preservation' is concerned this is

> *'not a legal right but an instinct...we ought not to argue that, because States or individuals are likely to behave in a certain way in certain circumstances, therefore they have a right to behave in that way'.* (47)

The law of war has traditionally constituted a stronghold of the extreme view of State Sovereignty or War Rights. Nevertheless we have seen how at St Petersburg, the Hague and subsequently, states have agreed to more and more restraints on how their right of self-defence is put into practice. Since 1945 there have been further developments in the International Humanitarian Law of Armed Conflict, and these have been increasingly complemented by the growth of two relatively recent areas of international law concerning *Human Rights and Environmental Protection.* The legal case against nuclearism rests most securely when correlated to all three currents.

Hiroshima 1945

Part Three: Nuclear Warfare and the Law

... exposed to radiation separately from my parents... I set out for the ruins of my house... a few bodies could be seen in the scorched field. Then, in a water tank... I saw a pile of bodies. Suddenly a terrible sight met me on the street... There stood the petrified body of a woman, with one leg lifted as though running, her baby tightly clutched in her arms. The memory will never leave me. Painting: Yasuko Yamagata , aged 17 in 1945.

A ten-megaton blast erupts into a sinister mushroom cloud above an atoll in the Pacific Ocean

Photo: L. Sirman

7. Criminality of nuclear use

The aim of this chapter will be to help peace people argue the case for the criminality of nuclear use, which provides the essence of the cases against nuclear threat and possession. It stands on the shoulders of excellent previous analyses, such as:

* *Report of the Nuclear Warfare Tribunal*
* *Writ of Summons* in the Dutch case of 20,000 plaintiffs versus the Netherlands government over its decision to accept Cruise missiles (1)
* Nagendra Singh's pioneering work in the 1950s, subsequently revised in the late 1980s while he was serving as President of the World Court
* *Nuclear Weapons and Scientific Responsibility* by Prof CG Weeramantry, who was subsequently elected to the ICJ following Singh's death.

Unlike many previous analyses which concentrate on the 'easy end' of the argument, such as massive counter-city strikes, this analysis will be more geared to the scenario of 'limited' battlefield uses. If its arguments are sound, they will apply all the more to counter-city strikes.

'No Express Prohibition' and the 'De Martens Clause'

Apologists for the nuclear weapon states often suggest that the use of nuclear weapons would be lawful in the absence of specific prohibitions against such a use. According to them, nuclear weapons are a weapon like any other, to be judged on the same footing as any other and in the specific circumstances of their use. (As we shall see they abandoned this position when it suited them while negotiating the 1977 Geneva Protocol I).

This reasoning is cogent in theory, but misleading in practice when the concrete effects of nuclear use are considered in the light of existing customary and treaty rules by which all nations are bound. The whole point is that nuclear 'weapons' are quantitatively and qualitatively different from other lawful weapon-systems (2). Those they half approximate to are banned in the 1972 Biological Weapons Convention (3) and the 1925 'Gas Protocol', which it is believed will shortly be strengthened by a Chemical Weapons Convention banning manufacture, possession, and deployment as well as use.

An explicit ban may be useful as a confirmation of the existing state of the law, but it would not be essential. In 1899 and again in 1907 the Hague Conventions included a 'catch-all' clause suggested by De Martens, a leading member of the Russian delegation, after whom the clause has been informally named. It was designed to prevent States attempting to justify barbaric new methods of slaughter not explicitly prohibited:

'Until a more complete code of the laws of war has been issued, the high contracting Parties deem it expedient to declare that, in cases not included in the Regulations adopted by them, the inhabitants and the belligerents remain under the protection and the rule of the principles of the law of nations, as they result from the usages established among civilized peoples, from the laws of humanity, and the dictates [1899 'requirements'] of the public conscience.'

(Preamble to 1907 Fourth Convention)

(The French has 'conscience publique' which is wider than conscience in English, denoting also public awareness).

The clause was relied on in post-WW2 war crimes trials, including the Krupp Trial, where the Tribunal described it as much more than a 'pious declaration', but rather 'the legal yardstick to be applied if and when the specific provisions of the Convention...do not cover specific cases occurring in warfare...' (4). Other versions of this clause were adopted in the 1949 Geneva Conventions (eg IV,158) and again in the far-reaching Additional Protocol I of 1977. Most recently the importance of the clause was affirmed in the *Nicaragua* case (5).

Since 1945 nuclearism has been repudiated in countless forums, declarations, petitions and actions of all kinds. It is impossible for the handful of nuclear nations to succeed in any claim that, although nuclear weapons are supposed to be normal weapons like any other, the question of their legal status should be interpreted against the grain of this massive, if indirect, body of evidence as to their moral and legal unacceptability.

IS NUCLEAR USE 'AN ESTABLISHED USAGE'?

The very fact that America was prepared to accept defeat in Vietnam rather than go nuclear could be said to indicate its fear of public reaction domestically and in the world community if it stooped to such uncivilised and inhumane depths.

This conclusion is reinforced by repeated *UN Resolutions*, including Resolution 1653 (XVI) of 1961 which recalled the UN's determination to protect 'succeeding generations from the scourge of war' (6). With only 20 votes against, it went on to declare:

'(a) The use of nuclear...weapons is contrary to the spirit, letter and aims of the UN and, as such, a direct violation of the Charter of the UN;

'(b) [Their use] would exceed even the scope of war and cause indiscriminate suffering and destruction to mankind and civilisation and, as such, is contrary to the rules of international law and to the laws of humanity;

'(c) [Their use] is in a war directed not against an enemy or enemies alone but also against mankind in general.' (7)

Many other UN Resolutions could be cited, including Resolution 2936 of 1972 (8), Resolution 75/38 of 1983 (9), and a series of resolutions originally tabled by India and resubmitted throughout the 1980s with increasing majorities (10). These reaffirmed 'that the use of nuclear weapons would be a violation of the UN Charter and a crime against humanity' and called for negotiations on an explicit treaty in which the parties would solemnly renounce the use or threat of nuclear weapons 'under any circumstances'.

The use of nuclear weapons is clearly neither a 'usage established among civilized peoples' nor does it reflect any 'general principle of law recognized by civilised nations'. Almost uniquely for any weapon system those who possess these devices have agreed to having their hands tied through a host of legally-binding promises. Among these specific 'express prohibitions' are a series of ad hoc restrictions on deployment made on a geographical basis:

Antarctic Treaty of 1959

Outer Space treaty of 1967

Latin American Nuclear-Free Zone Treaty of Tlatelolco of 1967

Ocean Floor Treaty of 1971

South Pacific Nuclear-Free Zone Treaty of Raratonga of 1985 (11);

To these we should also add Resolution 1652 (XVI) of 1961 and 2033 (XX) of 1965, calling on Member States to consider and respect Africa as a denuclearised zone; and a set of self-prohibitions with legal force in the shape of the *'Negative Security Assurances'* (NSAs) given by most of the nuclear nations to non-nuclear powers. China has promised non-use and non-threat-of-use 'against the non-nuclear countries and nuclear-free zones' as well as no first use against nuclear nations. By contrast France, the UK and the US have only promised non-use 'except in case of an attack on the UK ...or its allies by such a [non-nuclear] State in association or alliance with a nuclear-weapon State.' (UK formulation of June 1978)

The early 'De Martens' clause also speaks about the 'laws of humanity'. In domestic legal systems there is no 'express prohibition' on beating people to death with a golf club. But that does not mean that if we did so we could escape punishment. As a rule the law is not noun-focused, but deals in categories of action expressing relationships between people. Although there are plenty of lawful things which you could do with a golf club, there is nothing you could lawfully do with a nuclear 'weapon' (other than dismantle it). The laws of every nation taken individually prohibit killing and poisoning harmless people, and the 'laws of humanity' as a whole can scarcely be read to sanction massive loopholes whenever some new gadget is invented. 'The right to life is not lost as new methods of killing are invented.' (12)

1. Ban on Poison and Poisonous Weapons

This very ancient and universal customary prohibition has found expression in Hague Convention IV of 1907, Article 23 a (quoted earlier, page 61), Article 171 of the Treaty of Versailles and in the 1925 Geneva Convention which is commonly called the 'Gas Protocol' but which could equally well be called the 'Poison Protocol':

'Whereas the use in war of asphyxiating, poisonous or other gases, and of all analogous liquids materials or devices, has been justly condemned by the general opinion of the civilised world...'

(Preamble)

Legal and diplomatic authorities frequently ignore the fact that not only do nuclear 'weapons' contain poisonous materials, they also give off poisonous gas (e.g. radon) and cause an asphyxiating fire-storm.

Both Hague IV and the Geneva Protocol have been reaffirmed, in the Preamble to other treaties, in international declarations and at the UN. They are in complete conformity with national laws and are cited by the only judicial decision of a domestic court to have gone into the merits of the argument, the *Shimoda Judgement* of the Tokyo District Court in 1963. This branded the atomic bombing of Hiroshima and Nagasaki as war crimes (13). (All other domestic law cases have been decided on other grounds, e.g. that the issue was supposedly too political or difficult for the Courts to rule on (14)). The prohibition on the use of poisonous substances is contained in the military manuals of nuclear powers. Few more authoritative prohibitions exist in international law. It is universally binding on all nations.

Any claim that nuclear 'weapons' do not contain or spread poison would get short shrift from the International Court of Justice in the light of official reports and manuals circulated by the nuclear governments (15), and in the light of the official definition of an 'atomic weapon' annexed to the Paris Protocol of 1954 modifying and completing the 1948 *Brussels Treaty of Collaboration and Collective Self-Defence* (16) setting up the Western European Union:

> *'An atomic weapon is defined as any weapon which contains...radioactive isotopes and which...is capable of mass destruction, mass injury or mass poisoning.'*
>
> (Annex II, 1 a)

With the possible exception of the US, the great majority of jurists in every decade who have written about nuclear 'weapons' have classed them as in breach of the poison prohibition (17). This prohibition alone suffices to dispose of any idea of nuclear devices as normal war-fighting 'weapons'.

As poison-scattering devices nuclear 'weapons' thus fall foul of every one of the sources of law mentioned in Article 38 of the Statutes of the ICJ, with the possible exception of (c) General Principles of Law Recognised by Civilized Nations.

2. Ban on causing unnecessary, superfluous and aggravated suffering

The great customary principle underlying both the St Petersburg Declaration and Hague Regulation IV, 23(e) has subsequently been reaffirmed in numerous declarations and treaties including the 1977 Geneva Protocol I Additional to the Geneva Conventions of 1949:

'Article 35. Basic Rules...(2)

It is prohibited to employ weapons, projectiles and material and methods of warfare of a nature to cause superfluous injury or unnecessary suffering.'

Although the UK, US and France entered reservations purporting to exclude nuclear weapons from the scope of the treaty, they only advanced this claim in connection with 'new rules introduced' (UK) or 'the rules established' (US) by this Protocol (18).

Even restricting ourselves to a consideration of the effects on military personnel, it is clear that any survivors from a nuclear assault will not simply be put out of action, but will each day suffer new symptoms of gamma irradiation. These tortures will continue to effect them whether they have been disabled by blast and heat/fire effects, or captured, or whether peace has been declared - and are thus utterly pointless from a military point of view. Against the claim that inflicting such specific sufferings and perhaps rendering their death inevitable are only incidental to the main militarily-justified aim of 'disabling the greatest possible number of men', we can only quote the logic of the St Petersburg and Hague Conventions themselves: if military necessity is entertained in Hague IV 23(g) but not mentioned in Hague IV 22(e), then the rule is a categoric prohibition, irrespective of whatever new technologies and cries of 'military necessity' might arise.

In view of the overall cruelty of war this rule may appear absurd to both pacifists and nuclear 'realists' alike. But it exists. None of the current nuclear powers dissented from its existence and relevance in the pre-nuclear age and its legal standing is unimpaired in the nuclear era. It has the weight of judicial sanction (*Shimoda* case) and the support of a wide range of eminent jurists.

3. Prohibition on causing indiscriminate damage to harmless people

Deliberate terror attacks on civilians and civilian buildings are illegal no matter whether carried out with a hand grenade or a nuclear 'bomb'. The main legal problem in this area is the ease with which vast damage to civilians has been rationalised as being accidental or unintended, despite the general principle of law that people should be regarded as intending the consequences of their actions especially if their actions are known to be potentially risky and if the negative consequences are known to be likely (19).

Although obliged to spare civilian buildings 'as far as possible' (Hague, IV,27) the dominant State practice during WW2 brushed such protections aside on the basis that precise discrimination was impractical. Resulting civilian damage was deemed 'incidental' and 'not disproportionate' to the damage caused to (or merely intended for) 'vital military objectives'. The victims living in the rubble of Berlin or Tokyo may have deemed matters differently, and their suspicions were easily fanned when their leaders publicised (illegal) Allied bombing directives which listed 'enemy civilian morale' as a separate, not merely ancillary, objective of the bombing campaigns of 1943-45 (20).

The post-war world has seen many attempts to reaffirm the customary principle of non-combatant immunity, by the Red Cross, the Institute for International Law (21), and in resolutions at the United Nations, among them Res. 2675 (XXV) of 1970:

> ' *The General Assembly, affirms the following basic principles for the protection of civilian populations in armed conflicts:*
>
> 1. *Fundamental human rights, as accepted in international law and laid down in international instruments, continue to apply fully in situations of armed conflict.*
>
> 3. *In the conduct of military operations, every effort should be made to spare civilian populations from the ravages of war, and all necessary precautions should be taken to avoid injury, loss or damage to civilian populations.'* (22)

Some of these reaffirmations suffer from the difficulty inherent in seeking to tie the hands of military commanders using only vague self-assessed phrases about 'proportionality'. By far the most detailed attempt to spell out this concept is to be found in Additional Protocol I of 1977, but even here it proved impossible to eliminate certain verbal compromises allowing the military considerable leeway:

'Attacks which employ a method or means of combat the effects of which cannot be limited as required by this Protocol' are prohibited as 'indiscriminate'.

(Art. 51.4)

Area-bombing is outlawed along with attacks *'which may be expected to cause incidental loss of civilian life, injury to civilians...**excessive in relation to the concrete and direct military advantage anticipated**'.*

(51.5)

*'In the conduct of military operations, constant care shall be taken to spare the civilian population...those who plan or decide upon an attack shall take **all feasible precautions** in the choice of means and methods of attack with a view to avoiding, and in any event **minimizing**, incidental loss of civilian life...'*

(57.1 and .2)

Considering only the blast and fire effects of nuclear attacks, it appears that whether the general customary rule or its welcome elaboration in Additional Protocol 1 would suffice to prohibit an attack, would depend very much on the nature and location of that attack. Bombing cities would be a war crime, but tactical and battlefield uses might be legitimate.

On the other hand, once we take into account the radioactive fallout, it becomes well-nigh impossible to envisage any use of nuclear devices which would not harm civilians, if only through long-term diffusion of long-lasting isotopes in the atmosphere and food chains of the world. Even the 'cleanest' mini-nuke will cause very considerable death, genetic malformation, suffering and heartbreak sooner or later (23). This civilian damage may not appear very considerable in the hard eyes of nuclear generals and their well-funded legal apologists, but over one, ten, a hundred generations it must surely accumulate inexorably. Who is to say that the lives of people in the future are less real and precious than those of our generation? Who can be sure that by the time the half-life of plutonium 239 is reached (c.24,000 years) the total effects against succeeding generations will not easily outweigh any original death toll - however high, militarily focused and 'vital' that slaughter may once have been?

The Sri Lankan, Prof Christopher Weeramantry, has contrasted the tendency of the Western legal system 'to tailor legal concepts only in relation to the needs and desires of the current generation' with the attitude to intergenerational damage in traditional legal systems in Melanesia, China, and Africa where:

'The community participating in the legal system is thought of as being not only the living but those who have gone before and those who are yet to come.' (24)

If calling the civilian damage mere 'collateral side effects' is only possible on the basis of this-generational chauvinism, so too it seems inappropriate to use a pre-atomic model to talk of 'incidental damage'. This notion of 'incidental damage' derived from the practice of artillery gunners - and then bomb aimers - who sometimes unfortunately and accidentally missed targets, which would otherwise have been 'taken out surgically'. The poison-effects of nuclear devices cannot be used, pointed or reliably contained in space and time through improved aiming techniques. Damage to some civilians in this generation, and many in succeeding generations will occur inevitably and inexorably. **It is systemic to the course of action in question, and in no way 'incidental' to it.**

From this perspective let us now consider what specific treaty formulations of this customary norm are available to us - and the Court - for the anti-nuclear defence of our civilian estate.

3.a Geneva Conventions of 1949 (25)

Almost every nation in the world has made unconditional promises 'to respect and ensure respect for' the four Geneva Conventions 'in all circumstances' (Art.1). They create various categories of protected person whom States Parties undertake to treat with care and dignity: wounded, sick and shipwrecked members of the armed forces (I and II), prisoners of war (III) and 'civilians' (IV). Full-scale nuclear war would make it impossible for governments to discharge their protective duties, bury the dead and create hospital and safety zones. But even 'limited' nuclear strikes would spread poisonous fall-out which would be incompatible with the far-reaching obligations voluntarily assumed by states.

The usual text-book definition of 'specially protected civilians' quotes from only part of article IV, 4:

'Persons protected by the Convention are those who, at a given moment and in any manner whatsoever, find themselves, in case of a conflict or occupation, in the hands of a Party to the conflict or Occupying Power of which they are not nationals.' (26)

On this basis we may be forgiven for concluding that the Geneva Conventions are of limited value in defending against combat dangers.

However article 13 says:

'The provisions of Part II cover the whole of the populations of the countries in conflict, without any adverse distinction based, in particular, on race, nationality, religion or political opinion, and are intended to alleviate the sufferings caused by war.'

And further on in Part II we read:

'The wounded and sick, as well as the infirm, and expectant mothers, shall be the object of particular protection and respect...'

(Art.16)

'Persons regularly and solely engaged in the operation and administration of civilian hospitals...shall be respected and protected.'

(Art.20)

Part IV defines which acts 'against persons and property protected by the present Convention' amount to 'grave breaches' (i.e. war crimes). They include:

'wilful killing...inhumane treatment, wilfully causing great suffering or serious injury to body or health'

(Art.147 - which carries a 'military necessity' escape clause only in respect of destruction of property, as the French text makes clear) (27).

In view of the carnage of WW2, the diplomatic conference that created the Red Cross Conventions did not set its goals very high. It rejected a call for a clause explicitly outlawing nuclear weapons on the grounds that participants had convened to conclude a person-centred, not a weapons-centred, Convention. It was, admittedly, mostly concerned with the protection of civilians in occupied territories, which up to a point may influence the interpretation of genuinely ambiguous articles. But the plain meaning of texts should otherwise take precedence. The combined effect of these articles is to elevate expectant mothers, health workers and their charges into a special category of people to be protected wherever located in the warring countries, i.e. from the dangers of combat and not simply from the abuses of occupation.

Considering that pregnant women, their foetuses and the infirm are particularly vulnerable to the effects of gamma radiation, and also to fall-out carried in winds, foodchains and reproductive cells for thousands of years, even isolated battlefield nukes will 'wilfully cause serious injury to body or health', if only in the form of great mental anxiety.

If we receive junk mail telling us that we have been entered into a computerised draw, and stand one chance in fifty thousand of winning a range of cash prizes - are we not mildly pleased? But if someone tells us that the names of ourselves, our children and grandchildren, our friends and neighbours have all been entered into some arbitrary system of 'Radiation Roulette', then are we not indignant? We certainly don't feel 'objects of particular respect and protection'.

3.b Genocide Convention of 1948

Nuclear use would 'deliberately inflict on the group conditions of life calculated to bring about its physical destruction in whole or in part' and constitute a 'measure intended to prevent births within the group'. Although other parts of this definition in Article 2 are such as make its relevance to every kind of nuclear use a matter of controversy (destroying the group 'as such' with 'intent'), no such technicalities could be argued in the case of

3.c Nuremberg Principles of 1946, 1950

The principles of the 1945 Nuremberg Charter were unanimously affirmed by the General Assembly of the UN in 1946 (Res 95/I) and again by the International Law Commission in 1950. Their status in customary international law is thus beyond challenge. Article 6 creates international criminal liability for

> '(c) **Crimes Against Humanity:**
>
> *Murder...and other inhuman acts done against any civilian population, when ...done in connection with any war crime.'*

3.d Additional Protocol I

When convening the diplomatic conference which led to the 1977 Protocols, the ICRC circulated introductory comments on its draft treaty-text, which did contain restrictions on the use of certain conventional weapons.

'Problems relating to atomic, bacteriological and chemical warfare are subjects of international agreements or negotiations by governments and in submitting these draft Additional Protocols the ICRC does not intend to broach these problems.' (28)

On several occasions during the conference and on signing the US and UK made clear their 'understanding' that any new law made in the treaty would not apply to nuclear weapons. Most participants preferred to make what progress they could rather than risk a walk out. However these 'understandings' of the fact that the ICRC was not proposing to include any explicit atomic prohibition are not beyond challenge - and might well attract counter-reservations if either nation ratify the Protocols. Until then they are:

'obliged to refrain from acts which would defeat the object and purpose of the treaty'.

(Vienna Convention on the Interpretation of Treaties, Art.18)

In any case neither the general rule about taking care not to cause civilian casualties nor the Martens clause included in the treaty are 'new rules introduced' or 'established' by Protocol 1, whose legal authority continues to grow as more and more states accede to it.

3.e Universal Declaration of Human Rights of 1948 (29)

This authoritatively elaborates the references to human rights in the UN Charter. Although not binding as a treaty, its key provisions constitute 'general principles of law recognised by civilised nations'. It was adopted nem con in the General Assembly and has since been referred to in more formal treaties, such as the Helsinki Final Act of 1975. It binds Member States to 'secure the universal and effective recognition and observance' of the right to life (Art.3), equal protection of the law (Art.7) and conditions of living 'adequate for health and well-being', especially for mothers and children (Art.25). 'Everyone is entitled to a social and international order in which [these] rights and freedoms...can be fully realized.' (Art.28). The Rights to Life and Health are also set out in various regional declarations of Human Rights, but their most authoritative expression is in:

3.f The 1966 International Covenant on Civil and Political Rights (ICCPR) and the International Covenant on Economic, Social and Cultural Rights (ICESCR) (30)

These UN-adopted treaties remind nations of human rights standards which as members of the UN they have pledged to take joint and separate action to achieve:

'Everyone has the inherent right to life. This right shall be protected by law. No one shall be arbitrarily deprived of his right.'

(Art.6 of ICCPR - which States Parties may not derogate from even 'in time of public emergency which threatens the life of the nation' (Art.4).)

States Parties *'recognise the right of everyone to the enjoyment of the highest attainable standard of physical and mental health'* and commit themselves to steps necessary to lower the rate of stillbirths and infant mortality and improve environmental hygiene (Art.12 of ICESCR). The ICCPR set up a Human Rights Committee of 18 experts serving in their personal capacity, which has twice issued general comments on Article 6 which link the safeguarding of the Right to Life with the overcoming of the nuclear threat (31).

4. Prohibition on violating neutral nations

There is a general principle of law recognised by civilised nations called the 'comity of nations', which has also given rise to the law of peaceful co-existence or friendly relations (32). One aspect of this principle is the customary legal principle that a 'state may not legitimately permit its territory to be used in ways directly injurious to another state' (33) Another is the customary and treaty law of neutrality (34):

'The territory of neutral nations shall be inviolable.'
(Art.1 of 1907 Hague Convention V)

This treaty rule is merely declaratory of customary law independently binding on all nations, whether or not they have signed *Hague Convention V*. In a war long-standing neutral countries would be entitled to claim the rights of neutral nations, but so would other nations who were non-aligned in that particular conflict and were prepared to fulfill the duties of neutrality.

The *UN Charter* obliges states to refrain from *'the use of force against the territorial integrity...of any State'* (Art.4). *'Waging a war in violation of international treaties...and assurances'* constitutes a *'Crime against Peace'* according to Nuremberg Principle 6.a.

Since the direction of winds and currents cannot be exactly foretold, the possibility of neutral nations being visited by the immediate radioactive fallout plume of a nuclear detonation cannot be ruled out. In any case a proportion of the longer-lasting isotopes will inevitably find their way there in the long run. In Nuclear Tests Australia and New Zealand won interim relief ordering France not to violate their sovereignty with any further testing. As well as citing danger to their citizens in their application for this order, Australia and New Zealand also argued that any further explosion would infringe their 'decisional sovereignty' to set their own safety limits for radioactivity in the interests of their own citizens.

Earlier judicial decisions are also relevant. The judgment in the *Palmas Arbitration* included in the definition of one nation's sovereignty 'the obligation to protect within the territory the rights of other States, in particular their right to integrity and inviolability in peace and in war'. In the *Corfu Channel* case the ICJ held Albania liable for damage to British warships on the basis of

'certain general and well recognized principles, namely...every State's obligation not to allow, knowingly, its territory to be used for acts contrary to the rights of other States'.

UN Resolutions can also be cited as evidence of the continued vitality of the principle of third party immunity. In October 1961 the General Assembly declared:

'that both concern for the future of mankind and the fundamental principles of international law impose a responsibility on all States concerning actions which might have harmful biological consequences for the existing and future generations of peoples of other States, by increasing the levels of radio-active fall-out'.

(Res.1629 (XVI), passed *nem con* with 17 abstentions) (35).

All these arguments would apply all the more obviously if we were to consider the massive fallout effects, nuclear winter, etc resulting from large or even medium-scale nuclear war.

5. Prohibition on Causing Severe Damage to the Natural Environment

It is a commonplace that radioactivity is no respecter of frontiers. For obvious reasons the issue of transboundary pollution found no place in classical international law. Nevertheless classical principles have been extended to cover this problem in the Trail Smelter (36) and Lake Lanoux Arbitrations (37) of 1941 and 1957 respectively:

'No State has the right to use or permit the use of its territory in such a manner as to cause injury by fumes in or to the territory of another or the properties therein, when the case is of serious consequence and the injury is established by clear and convincing evidence.'

(Trail Smelter, p 1965)

The preamble of the 1963 *Partial Test Ban Treaty* expresses the desire 'to put an end to the contamination of man's natural environment by radioactive substances' (38).

In Article 1 the Parties undertake:

'to prohibit, prevent, and not to carry out any nuclear weapon test explosion, or any other nuclear explosion, at any place under its jurisdiction or control:

a) in the atmosphere;...or under water...

b) in any other environment if such explosion causes radioactive debris to be present outside the territorial limits of the State under whose jurisdiction or control such explosion is conducted.'

Another important indication of the growing ecological concern of the world community was the Declaration issued by the Stockholm Conference on the Environment of 1972 (39), whose legal significance was confirmed unanimously by the General Assembly in Res 2996 (XXVII):

'All States have the responsibility to ensure that activities within their jurisdiction or control do not cause damage to the environment of other states or of areas beyond the limits of national jurisdiction' (40).

(This Principle 21 was subsequently incorporated in Article 30 of the Charter of Economic Rights and Duties of States of 1974) (41).

The 1977 Protocol I contains two rules which had not previously been formulated in a treaty before:

'Methods and Means of Warfare: Article 35 - Basic Rules.....:

3. *It is prohibited to employ methods or means of warfare which are intended, or may be expected, to cause widespread, long-term and severe damage to the natural environment.*

'Article 55:1. Care shall be taken to protect the environment against widespread and severe damage...[which may be expected] to prejudice the health or survival of the population.'

In front of the Ichino-torii (shrine-gate), about 700 meters south of the hypocenter, Nagasaki, August 10 1945. Photo Yosuke Yamahata

We have already mentioned the dubious minority claims of the US, UK and France concerning the supposed non-applicability of 'new rules' to the use of nuclear 'weapons'. Even if in 1977 the rules concerning the natural environment had been 'new rules', we maintain:

* that the existence of these above-mentioned official formulations (from 1963, 1972 and 1977 itself) is evidence of an emerging customary norm in line with the dictates of the public conscience;
* and that since 1977 this norm **has emerged** into a fully fledged binding rule of international law which stands on its own account.

As evidence for this view we could cite :

* 1982 *Convention on the Law of the Sea* (42), which laid down various principles governing areas of the seas beyond the jurisdiction of any nation. As 'the common heritage of mankind', use of this area is to be 'exclusively for peaceful purposes' and must pay due regard to protection of the marine environment and human life (Arts. 136,141,145,146);
* The second *Helsinki Accords* also oblige signatories to use technologies which protect the environment in the interests of future generations;
* many other declarations, UN Resolutions, etc have all added weight to this rule of environmental responsibility.

If in 1977 when Additional Protocol I was being drafted it could not yet have been said that Articles 35 and 55 were merely declaratory of an independently existing customary norm, the same is not true today. Moreover this rule may well be considered to have emerged into the category of most fundamental over-riding and peremptory rules known as *jus cogens*, which is binding on all members of the international community, irrespective of whether they have signified their consent so to be bound, and hence irrespective of any reservations they may have once made.

6. Prohibition to Destroy Valuable 'Civilian Objects'

Every nuclear explosion gives off a powerful electro-magnetic pulse which disables electronic equipment in a very wide arc (43). For example a 'bomb' detonated in the Eastern Mediterranean Sea might well put vital equipment out of action in the hospitals and libraries, etc of Cairo. This would violate:

* *Hague Conventions* IV 27 and IX 5 of 1907;
* *Geneva Convention* IV 18 of 1949;
* 1954 *Hague Convention for the Protection of Cultural Property in the Event of Armed Conflict,* whose preamble expresses the conviction that:

  'damage to cultural property belonging to any people whatsoever means damage to the cultural heritage of all mankind, since each people makes its contribution to the culture of the world' (44);
* and the 1977 *Additional Protocol I,* Articles 52 and 12 of which codify the pre-existing customary rule of general protection of civilian objects and medical units.

Depending on their location and scale, nuclear explosions may also violate other provisions of the Humanitarian Law of Armed Conflict codified in the 'Red Cross' *Protocol I*:

* protection of objects indispensable to the survival of the civilian population (Art.54)
* protection of works and installations containing dangerous forces such as dams, dykes and civil nuclear power plants (Art.56)

Likewise, many nuclear contingency plans contemplate use of such kinds and/or on such a scale as must inevitably violate so-called 'second generation' human rights which pertain to whole societies: e.g. Right to Development, Right to Peace or the Right of Peoples to Survive featured in Art.20 of the African Charter of Human and Peoples' Rights (45).

Reprisals use of nuclear devices

Customary international law provides that when one nation makes a material violation of a treaty, the other nation may also break free of its restrictions. Hence nations signing a treaty often state that their adherence is 'subject to reciprocity'. For example, many countries made reservations to the 1925 Geneva Protocol in line with that of France:

> 'The said Protocol shall *ipso facto* cease to be binding on [France] in regard to any enemy State whose armed forces or whose Allies fail to respect the prohibitions laid down in the Protocol.' (46)

One implication of this is that when subject to Iraqi poison attacks, Iran could, in principle, have legally resorted to the use of poison gas against Iraq (but see other conditions to follow). This makes the 1925 Protocol effectively a No First Use agreement.

There is also a rule of customary law which sanctions **wartime belligerent reprisals: otherwise illegal acts done in response to a prior breach of international law by the other side.** By this definition those who defend the legality of nuclear use should logically be prevented from arguing **both** that nuclear 'weapons' are normal war-fighting weapons like any other **and** that their use is to deter the other side from violating international law, since they could be used in a reprisals mode. In practice they prefer to keep both purported options open.

Reprisals are often the gateway to serious abuse and even breakdown of international law, which might well indicate that this is one more 'belligerent right' which should be abolished. On the other hand the most powerful nations argue that it would hardly be conducive to the rule of law if unscrupulous nations could break the rules with impunity and the most law-abiding nations always lost. Hence the international community has settled for an approach which deploys 'just war' criteria to impose conditions on the lawful exercise of the right of reprisals in wartime:

* it must be **in response to a serious violation** in the way the other side is conducting the war (having been attacked is not enough);
* it must be **as a last resort** - and should generally be preceded by an unsuccessful protest which contains details of the complaint and a formal warning.

* **it must be proportionate to the original violation.** Most experts concede that reprisals don't have to be identical in kind and severity, which makes estimating proportionality difficult. There is little support amongst jurists for the view that since a reprisal action is shaped with the goal of influencing the future behaviour of the opponent, considerably greater violence may be apt or 'proportional' for its task of deterring the enemy from any further violation of the laws of war (47).

* all agree that reprisals should be calculated and applied judiciously, if necessary by stages. The sole justification for reprisals derives from the aim of inducing the opponent to step back into conformity with the laws of war, not revenge or 'punishment' (48).

The classical doctrine of reprisals was evolved in relation to a two-actor model of infringement and response leading to renewed respect for the law. 'Reprisals are used between nation and nation, in order to do themselves justice when they cannot otherwise obtain it' (49). However the poison-dimension of nuclear devices cannot be squashed into this old model. Especially since WW2 a series of further restrictions have been placed on the exercise of the right of reprisal which reflect the fact that as a rule we are no longer dealing with an affair between two sovereigns:

1. In its *Third Report on State Responsibility* the UN's International Law Commission quotes with approval from jurists who have suggested that the 'otherwise-illegal' nature of a reprisal action must not extend to committing an act which violates a peremptory rule of customary international law, *jus cogens* (50). Certain 'supreme exigencies of civilization and humanity' must override the sovereignty of individual states, no matter how aggrieved they feel.

2. The ILC also suggests that in responding to a provocation by state B, state A should not overthrow a rule which also binds it to states C to Z (51). Thus using the Iran-Iraq analogy, the kind of poisonous device which Iran might be permitted to use in retaliation or in reprisal should not be such as would poison Turkey, Jordan, Saudi Arabia, etc. Like the obligations to refrain from invasions and genocide, the obligation not to spread poison is an obligation **which states owe to all other states and which all other states have an interest in seeing upheld** (52).

3. The ILC also cites (p 17):

   * the peacetime reprisals case of the *Naulilaa arbitration* between Portugal and Germany in respect of killings in Angola, in which it was decided that for a reprisal to be lawful it should be 'limited by the demands of humanity' (p 1026), and

   * the 1934 declaration of the prestigious Institute for International Law which likewise declared that in the exercise of reprisals 'a State must abstain from any measure of compulsion which would be contrary to the laws of humanity and the demands of the public conscience' - echoes of De Martens.

4. The concern of the world community to raise certain values and norms beyond the reach of reprisals and counter-reprisals is also reflected in the *Vienna Convention on the Interpretation of Treaties* of 1969. Article 60 provides that Parties specially affected by a material breach of a treaty may invoke this breach as a ground for terminating or suspending the operation of a treaty in whole or in part 'in the relations between itself and the defaulting State'. However this does not apply

'to provisions relating to the protection of the human person contained in treaties of a humanitarian character, in particular to provisions prohibiting any form of reprisals against persons protected by such treaties'

(Art.60.5)

Treaties covered by this paragraph clearly include

* Geneva Convention IV of 1949 which the parties 'undertake to respect...in all circumstances' (Art.1) and which explicitly prohibits 'reprisals against protected persons and their property' (Art.33);

* Hague Convention of 1954 prohibits 'any act directed by way of reprisals against cultural property' (Art.4.4);

* Additional Protocol I of 1977 which prohibits reprisals against military and civilian medical units, religious personnel, aid workers (Part 2), civilians (Art.51.6), civilian objects (Art.52.1), cultural objects (Art.53), objects indispensable to the survival of the civilian population (Art.54), the natural environment (Art.55.2) and works and installations containing dangerous forces (Art.56.4). (Not all of these were 'new rules');

* and various Human Rights treaties, which, besides, often contain provisions ringfencing our non-combatant right to life against erosion even in a war.

In other words, harmless human beings are not to be wasted simply because one or two bullies are fighting and one or both is/are blinded by lust for battle. Nor may powerful people take out their frustrations with other powerful people on defenceless children, the unborn, etc. Belligerents rights are 'not unlimited' and these restrictions on reprisals and retaliation exactly conform to 'the laws of humanity' in the sense of humanitarian moral feeling, and of the way this is enshrined in the ordinary criminal code of every nation.

Nuclear retaliation is a contradiction in terms: all nuclear use inevitably involves 'first-strike' (first-poison) against harmless people unconnected with any armed conflict. Since the vast majority of its victims will not have committed any grave breaches of the laws of war, a nuclear 'reprisal' is also a contradiction in terms.

●●●●●●●●●●●●●●●●●●●●●●●●●●●●●●●●

We have argued the criminality of 'ordinary' nuclear use on six related but different grounds, most of which apply to rule out reprisals use also. Even if we are mistaken concerning one or two of these grounds, are we mistaken in respect of all of them? Yet this is what the legal defenders of nuclearism must argue! (53)

In written submissions and arguments before the Court, the nuclear nations are likely to paint highly untypical scenarios in which so-called 'low yield' 'clean bombs' are accurately directed against vital military targets with 'insignificant' or 'purely hypothetical' fallout-effects portrayed as incapable of measurement or prediction. In addition the UK, US, Israelis, etc will not hesitate to locate these tactical reprisal-attacks within wider 'strategic' scenarios:

If that battleship or this tank column is not nuked immediately, then the lamp of freedom on earth will eventually be extinguished, for the other side are intent on taking over the world! These well-armed, fanatical and ruthless totalitarians are on the verge of defeating the last centre of serious resistance. All the human values for which the West has always fought hang in the balance. Surely in such a situation it would be necessary to scatter a little poison in order to Save Civilization As We Know It?

The rationale of averting world domination was acidly brushed aside by George Schwarzenberger in 1958:

'As, in a divided world, each side is bound to accuse the other of this ultimate design [of imposing world domination], the function of this asserted right or duty is to provide in advance and indiscriminately, both sides with semi-legal justification for the use of the 'ultimate deterrent'.

Even if some members of the World Court were inclined to entertain some version of pro-nuclear special pleading as a theoretical possibility, we are confident that the majority will be well aware of

* the utter implausibility of this overall scenario;
* the current ratios of large/middle-sized nuclear 'weapons' to so-called 'small' ones' in the armouries of nuclear nations;
* the actual location of most 'vital military objectives', the proximity of most of them to centres of population, and winds blowing towards neutral countries;
* the impermissibility of allowing the gaps in our scientific knowledge to be read as a licence for inflicting risks on others in this and future generations: we civilians too are entitled to have **our** 'worst case scenarios' taken seriously until disproved by convincing research!

But there are other reasons too why the Court should be most reluctant to permit even the tiniest loophole for reprisals use, reasons to do with considerations of global policy. The original doctrine of reprisals grew up as self-help law-enforcement in the absence of the possibility of mobilising the world community in order to bring speedy and effective sanctions to bear against a serious violator of the laws of war, genocide, etc. In our global village, when the Security Council can be convened within hours, the alternative is no longer 'letting the violator get away with it'. But so long as the abstract possibility of reprisals use remains, powerful nations will continue to look to arms to guarantee their own security, rather than developing international arrangements for the vindication of all our common security. (54)

Moreover, the notion of reprisals is based on a model of two equally matched adversaries. But the World Court, being an organ of the UN, has equal, if not greater responsibilities towards the majority of nations who are smaller, poorer or less able to resort to high-tech reprisals against military targets. This global majority has an urgent interest in superseding the era of law-enforcement through ad hoc reprisals, by a non-discriminatory and non-arbitrary system of stopping grave breaches of the law of war, one based on prompt and consistent solidarity with all victimised nations.

8. Illegality of nuclear threats

Instead of writing of 'use' in the last chapter, we should perhaps have referred to 'poison-scattering explosions in wartime', and this for two reasons:

* for us civilians the dominant feature of nuclear devices is the danger of radioactive poisoning, and poison cannot be 'used' or directed, only the blast effects;
* threatening is also an active and destructive 'use' for nuclear weapons, witness Truman's 'atomic diplomacy' to get the USSR out of Northern Iran in 1946 (55), or Kennedy's during the Cuban Missile Crisis.

'The notion, common to nearly all Americans, that 'no nuclear weapons have been used since Nagasaki' is mistaken. Again and again, generally in secret from the American public, US nuclear weapons **have** been used...in the precise way a gun is used when you point it at someone's head in a confrontation, whether or not the trigger is pulled.' (56)

The UN Charter obliges Member States:

* *'to settle their international disputes by peaceful means in such a manner that international peace and security, and justice, are not endangered'* (Art.2.3)
* to *'refrain in their international relations from the threat ... of force against the territorial integrity or political independence of any State, or in any manner inconsistent with the Purposes of the UN'* (Art.2.4).

Since ample means exist for nations to resolve disputes peacefully and/or refer perceived dangers to the Security Council, the simplest and most cogent reading of the Charter is to say that threats to use any kind of force may only be issued where these other means have been tried and found wanting. Moreover any conditional threat or ultimatum must conform to the strictly defensive requirements of Article 51.

'If the promise is to resort to force in conditions in which no justification for the use of force exists, the threat itself is illegal.' (57)

Moreover the warning should only involve force of such a kind that it can be focused, so that the threat-element works on the minds of the potential invaders. It must not cause insecurity among neutral nations and civilian populations generally, who have a right to 'freedom from fear' (58)

By and large the majority of nations, particularly Southern nations, favour a restrictive view of the circumstances in which force may be used or threatened. This view was supported in the *Nicaragua* case and all the more powerfully since the ICJ restricted itself to pre-Charter law.

However a minority - with the US, UK and Israel to the fore - interpret the Charter as if Article 51 had not set conditions on the 'inherent' customary right of self-defence. According to this school of thought, force may be used in 'anticipatory self-defence' in the light of a reasonably founded view of imminent attack by the other side - or even of potential threat in the case of the Israeli air raid against Iraq's nuclear reactor in 1981! Numerous other flagrant abuses of this (in any case controversial) doctrine of 'anticipatory self-defence' could be cited, e.g. German invasion of Poland in 1939, Soviet invasion of Czechoslovakia in 1968, US invasion of Grenada in 1983.

In the context of modern war there is a tremendous premium placed on getting in the first blow, e.g. Israel's destruction on the ground of most of Egypt's airforce in 1967. When accompanied during crises by their recipient's knowledge of the issuing nation's belief in 'anticipatory self-defence', threats of force are just as likely to incite and magnetise attack as they are to deter and prevent it. Even Sadurska, who believes threats can help deter violence, has to admit that 'this is a precarious game' and that 'an environment in which threats of force are regularly used is likely to be very unstable' (59).

Instability will be all the greater when both parties deploy extremely accurate nuclear missiles capable of hitting nuclear missile silos (and thereby scattering double the poison in huge groundbursts). Even if nuclear devices were otherwise lawful 'weapons', the argument from instability would alone amount to a powerful policy consideration in favour of banning threats of force involving nuclear systems, or at very least all such threats issued prior to the occurrence of an armed attack.

Throughout the 1980s, the General Assembly of the UN has linked threat and (explosive) use in a *Draft Convention* on which it has repeatedly pressed the Conference on Disarmament to begin negotiations:

'Article 1: The States Parties to this Convention solemnly undertake not to use or threaten to use nuclear weapons under any circumstances.' (60)

This resolution has been routinely opposed by NATO countries who argue that nuclear 'weapons' could be used lawfully and hence that the deterrent threat of their legitimate use would also be lawful. Although NATO argues that it would never use nuclear weapons except in response to aggression, unlike China it refuses to make a legally binding declaration renouncing 'first use'. Its whole proclaimed policy of 'deterrence' depends on holding open for itself the option of going nuclear first.

However ever since Grotius international law has sought to keep a reasonably watertight compartment between *jus ad bellum* and *jus in bello*. After all, every nation thinks it has 'God on its side' and how is the ordinary soldier to know who really attacked first? Thus the mere fact of being in the right against invading nation B does not entitle defending nation A to 'fight dirty' in reply. Nor does it entitle nation A to put itself in the wrong towards nations C to Z. Any reasonable interpretation of Article 2.4 of the Charter excludes 'first strike' (read: first poison) threats against the territorial integrity and citizens of third party nations.

Against the claim that only accurate 'limited' tactical strikes would be threatened, the US Lawyers Committee on Nuclear Policy has argued:

*'Any use of a 'clean' tactical nuclear weapon, **assuming such a thing were possible**, would not be effective as a deterrent. On the other hand, strategic or theatre-level nuclear war would most likely destroy the territorial integrity and political independence of a target state, and it would be inconsistent with other purposes of the United Nations, such as preserving the right to life, safeguarding the environment,etc. Therefore, the threat of use of nuclear weapons as a deterrent constitutes a violation of Article 2.4.'* (61).

Proponents of nuclear 'deterrence' also argue the legality of the threat of nuclear retaliation against their prior use by the other side or to deter the enemy from continuing to perpetrate comparable war crimes committed in other ways. If the case made in the preceding chapter succeeded in plugging the Selective Reprisals loophole, then NATO cannot threaten lawful nuclear reprisals either.

Of course proponents of the 'deterrence' ideology then switch the argument to claim that nuclear weapons are not deployed for war but to prevent war. Even if the use would be poisonous and disproportionate to the military objective sought, it is claimed that the threat of use and all accompanying preparations may still be morally and legally justified (62). The main ground for this view is that in the light of the alleged absence of alternative ways of preventing nuclear war, such a threat has worked.

This is a highly dubious claim. In 1913 gunpowder could be said to have 'kept the peace' in Europe since 1871. The probability of reprisals may well have helped to deter Germany from the combat use of gas in World War 2, and many people consider that it would have been a much more potent factor in Hitler's mind than either his own painful memories from World War 1 or the existence of the 1925 'Gas Protocol'. This impression is strengthened when we correlate the massive US and French violations of the 1929 Prisoners of War Convention in 1945/46 with the beginning of the time when Germany could no longer retaliate against Allied POWs (63).

Opponents of 'deterrence' do not need to deny the apparent efficacy of threats of reprisals for short periods and in specific contexts. What we can and do deny is that a law-enforcement regime based on reprisals is stable in the long term, or wise, or just, or that it should be continued to be supported given the alternative law-enforcement regime of the UN system for common security, dispute resolution, law-enforcement action, and sanctions (64).

As the Security Council itself declared in Res. 188 condemning a UK (peacetime) reprisal action in the Fort Harib incident of 1964:

'reprisals are incompatible with the purposes and principles of the United Nations'.

Of course every legal system involves a deterrent threat or warning: if you break the law, we will lock you up. This kind of conditional threat is quite different from the man who says 'If you damage my motor car, I will damage yours', let alone 'If you burgle my house, I will kill you, burn your children and poison the neighbourhood'. Even if some domestic legal systems might exonerate the first sort of threat in exceptional circumstances, no societies could tolerate the latter. Thus 'general principles of law recognised by civilised nations' and general considerations of public policy combine with the UN Charter and Resolutions to render nuclear threats unlawful.

What of the State Practice argument? At least one of the nuclear weapons states has made crisis-threats - backed by threatening deployments - on about 20 known occasions (65). That they are often issued in secret is itself significant. A tiny minority of other nations subscribe to systems of nuclear deterrence involving latent threats. Only China has made legally-self-binding promises of no first use and never to threaten to use its nuclear capacity against non-nuclear countries and nuclear-free zones. Since most of these nuclear nations exercise a permanent right of veto on the Security

Council, it is illegitimate to argue from nuclear threats having gone unpunished to try to establish some purported legitimacy for these threats. One could as well argue that a bankrobber with an accomplice in the local police station has not been breaking the law! Or that since torture exists in many countries, it is 'permitted' by international law.

Ranged against the nuclear threat are 140 countries who regularly call for use and threat to be explicitly outlawed in a short specific treaty.

Some jurists have argued that the law in any area should take into account the practice of the 'leading nations' who are 'most involved' in that area. The ICJ has endorsed the 'specially affected interest' doctrine in the context of the *North Sea Continental Shelf* cases (para 73). But we must protest with all our power against this reasoning being extended to atomic warfare (66) - as if 'having nuclear weapons' was to be equated with 'having a coastline'. If anything one could say that **not** being in the position to issue nuclear threats gives the position of countries special weight in this area of the law. This would be even more the case if non-nuclear countries were to couple their renunciation of any policy designed to equip them with the means to make such a threat with an *opinio juris* statement of obligation - 'we are renouncing such a course of action as illegal'.

'The practice of the world's most powerful and influential nations in accumulating nuclear weapons and threatening to use them cannot be lightly dismissed, but neither can it be considered to have created new rules of customary international law permitting their deployment and use. As Arbess has argued, such a view 'fundamentally ignores the concept of law as an enterprise tailored toward the realization of certain basic, politically immutable values [including] the sanctity of human life and the principle of minimizing losses and suffering in armed conflict which constitute the basis of the entire law of war'. Legal principles cannot be derived from practice which disregards those values.' (67)

Finally let us check the criminality of nuclear threats against certain 'principles of humanity' derived from moral philosophy. Because something is claimed to 'work' is not a sufficient justification.

'It is immoral and illegal for a state to imply its willingness to violate principles of humanitarian law to impose substantial and unacceptable costs on any potential adversary. If soldiers are trained to torture prisoners and terrorize the civilian population ..., it may make other states wary of a conflict with such an adversary, assuming the threat was credible.' (68)

By way of analogy George Delf has suggested that tying babies to car bumpers would undoubtedly deter accidents and speeding. The perverse 'rationality' of nuclear deterrence then goes to harness its own moral unthinkability to strengthen its assertion that nuclear threats should not be judged on their contents, solely in terms of their function. The argument goes that however immoral and illegal it would be to carry out such threats, it is not immoral and illegal to utter them, because uttering them with credibility is supposed to ensure that they never have to be carried out. This is the vocabulary of Orwell's 'War is Peace' or Reagan's MX missile system 'the Peacemaker'.

It is contrary to natural reason to permit any course of action to be judged in terms of its own alleged infallibility. All policies sometimes backfire: opponents may be insane or imagine a bluff. All immoral threats lower the moral watertable from which humanity will continue to need to draw sustenance in the future. At very most such a distinction between threat and execution could only justify 'deterrence' on the most minimal basis, as a temporary expedient and on the condition that alternative security policies are sought with the utmost urgency.

Even if we concede that the primary intention of what could be termed nuclear 'deterrorism' is to avoid war, the policy makes no sense in its own terms without also implying another secondary intention, however conditional, that is deeply corrupt and corrupting for individuals and societies alike. As an American Jesuit has argued:

'The taproot of violence in our society is our intent to use nuclear weapons. Once we have agreed to that, all other evil is minor in comparison. Until we squarely face the question of our consent to use nuclear weapons, any hope of large-scale improvement of public morality is doomed to failure.' (69)

We should not proceed one inch down the slippery slope of arguing that the intention to wage nuclear war is less immoral than the action itself. General principles of law and humanity surely render nuclear threats, whether of 'first use' or 'retaliation', as illegal as it would be to carry out those threats. Nuclear warfare doctrine cannot be squashed into the old pre-nuclear two-actor model of conventional deterrence. Just as nuclear explosions pollute the physical atmosphere between states, nuclear threats poison the social and spiritual atmosphere. They terrorise us all.

Members of Scottish Christian CND led by the Rev. Maxwell Craig, general secretary of 'Action of Churches Together in Scotland', marching to present a petition and evidence to the Lord Advocate, arguing that Trident is in breach of Scottish law and of international law, and requesting a formal, legal inquiry into the truth of this allegation. March 1992.

Emblem of the International Court of Justice (ICJ) at the UN Headquarters, New York

UN photo: 173709/Saw Lwin

9. Legal status of nuclear preparations

The term 'nuclear possession' prevents clear thought. Even in the case of China we are not talking of purely inert possession as if it was an old shotgun kept under the bed for many years, with some ammunition in the back of the sock drawer. Most nuclear 'possession' is more akin to a man striding down the street with a rifle that is both cocked and loaded, which he brandishes in the direction of alarmed passers by. Nuclear warheads are not kept secretly in caves far from the front line and remote from other forms of military hardware. They are known to be **actively deployed** by being attached to delivery vehicles that are interconnected with sophisticated command, control, communication and intelligence systems (70)

In this section we shall proceed on the assumption that people don't buy lawn-mowers so as never to cut the grass. We shall consider manufacture, testing, acquisition, storing and maintenance of the lawn-mower in the light of common sense - that someone has some intention to cut grass and is making various kinds of preparations thereto. Indeed the reliability argument advanced on behalf of nuclear testing clearly indicates that the organisers believe the equipment must be ready for effective use at any time.

'Concerning nuclear weapons, it is submitted that there can be no justification for placing responsibility for manufacture in a different legal category from responsibility for use. The only difference is the difference between the commission of a crime and preparation to commit a crime.

'If a particular article is considered damaging to society, its manufacture is banned as well as its use. This is the case, for instance, with explosives and narcotics. It is an offence to manufacture the first, and it is an offence to grow the plants that yield the latter. Can the most damaging articles in human history - nuclear weapons - attract a different principle?' (71)

Dangers of accidents and abuse

One of the most crucial general principles of law is that the safety of the people is the supreme law. Of course the nuclear powers also cite this maxim to justify nuclear preparations! But every human endeavour may fail, not least 'deterrence' (72). Every technical system may break down - witness Chernobyl and the space shuttle disaster. And when nuclear 'fail-safe systems' fail they fail in a deadly fashion. Even if all the military personnel involved with these technologies had secret plans to enforce the law by arresting their superiors if they were ever 'ordered to fire' (incited to scatter poison (73)), the mere existence of nuclear 'weapons' is a source of wholly reasonable insecurity to millions.

RISK ASSESSMENT

The science of risk analysis calculates risks in terms of **how bad an outcome would be if it occurred** times **how small its likelihood is of coming about**. Thus we may risk a one in five chance of missing a local bus to see a friend, because we can always get the next bus and our friend won't mind too much. On the other hand if we were worried about missing some vital appointment (worse outcome), we would want to allow plenty of time (reducing the likelihood of the negative outcome).

If we talk of only a single nuclear warhead, it is obvious that it has a certain finite risk of being stolen by terrorists (unofficial ones); another of being launched at a city by a madman; another of exploding or leaking by accident. These outcomes are extremely grave, therefore we would want to insist that every precaution possible is taken. If it is linked to command and control computers and delivery systems it becomes harder to predict which bit of the total 'weapon'-system might go wrong and guard against such a likelihood, however small it may be. When we consider several nuclear devices, their systems and personnel, the likelihood of something eventually going wrong increases considerably. And the outcome too could be even worse, e.g. warheads setting each other off, or being interpreted as a hostile attack, or the Dr Strangelove scenario of some fundamentalist commander sending his planes against the Anti-Christ. (74)

When we consider 50,000 such devices, or even the 5,000 in Boris Yeltsin's minimal-deterrence arithmetic, the risk equation changes again, both in scale and quality. The more warheads, the greater the statistical certainty of one or more such 'peacekeepers' being sooner or later dropped, stolen, struck by lightning, etc (75). There is also a small finite likelihood of all-out nuclear war. This would spell nuclear winter, utter catastrophe, conceivably even the end of most forms of life on earth. No more humans, human objects, values or laws (76). And no more Courts to pronounce after the event.

Because the end of the game is not a number in the game, the outcome of nuclear winter cannot be assigned a finite value (however extreme) in any rational calculation. Therefore no finite level of likelihood, even (for the sake of argument) one in a million, can compensate for an infinitely bad outcome. The likelihood has to be zero. (77) Which implies disarmament down to zero and beyond (verified destruction of manufacturing capacities). (78)

Even if certain nations had a right to 'take the risk', international law could never justify them inflicting such a risk (79).

So long as hostile nuclear devices exist there is a danger of miscalculation, the breakdown of deterrence, warning shots functioning as incitements to 'get our retaliation in first', one-off reprisals leading to a spiral of counter-reprisals, and so on. Even if it were somehow lawful to detonate nuclear 'weapons' in highly restricted circumstances, how could we be certain that governments would respect such legal restrictions? Thus in addition to the argument from accidents, we can deploy the argument from the dangers of 'abuse'.

Britain in 1930 argued for a blanket ban on chemical weapons, against those who suggested that certain uses of gas wouldn't be so very deadly:

'The dangers of recognising any categories of permitted gases, and thus sanctioning the manufacture of the necessary equipment for using them are obvious and great, so that, it is submitted, the Society of States has adopted the right policy in endeavouring to extirpate this mode of warfare in toto' (80).

The need for a blanket ban in cases where dangers of abuse are socially unacceptable is a general principle of law in domestic legal systems, and has been confirmed on the international plane in *Corfu Channel*, when the ICJ disallowed Britain's claimed right of preventive operations in foreign territory in its dispute with Albania over illegally placed mines (81).

Crime against Peace, Crime against Humanity

If we regard possession of nuclear systems in a realistic light as being part of some kind of preparations to use them, then we have to view the leaders of all nuclear weapon states as guilty of **crimes against peace,** defined in the Nuremberg Principles as:

'6.a.(i) Planning, preparation, initiation, or waging of a war of aggression or a war in violation of international treaties, agreements or assurances;

(ii) Participation in any common plan or conspiracy for the accomplishment of any of the acts mentioned under (i).' This is the crux of the argument against nuclear possession, testing and other preliminaries to actual use. Nobody could try to belittle the well-established status as customary and binding law of the *Nuremberg Principles*, least of all the main nuclear powers who originally drafted the *Nuremberg Charter* (82).

These criminal preparations have already led to the deaths and maiming of countless civilians around the world - regardless of what stage of the nuclear cycle they have taken place (83). Further, these preparations have constituted a cruel blight over the psychic and spiritual horizons of millions, as seen in children's nuclear nightmares, or in the unprecedented sense of oppression stemming from our loss of a sense of an assured future for humankind (84).

On the assumption that nuclear use would fall under the scope of the UN *Genocide Convention* of 1948 (see page 75), then nuclear preparations constitute the crimes of Conspiracy to commit genocide (Art III b) or Complicity in genocide (Art.III.e), which the UN and its members have undertaken to prevent and to punish 'whether committed in time of peace or in time of war' (Art.I)

The threat posed by the very existence of nuclear weapons has concerned the UN Human Rights Committee. In 1982 it stated:

'The Committee considers that states have the supreme duty to prevent wars, acts of genocide and other acts of mass violence causing arbitrary loss of life. Every effort they make to avert the danger of war, especially thermo-nuclear war,...would constitute the most important condition and guarantee for the safeguarding of the right to life.' (85)

Unusually, the Committee returned to this theme in another unanimous 'general comment' in 1985:

'4....It is evident that the designing, testing, manufacture, possession and deployment of nuclear weapons are among the greatest threats to the right to life which confront mankind today...

'6. The production, testing, possession, deployment and use of nuclear weapons should be prohibited and recognized as crimes against humanity.' (86)

Note that by adding the word 'recognized' the Committee sought to avoid giving ammunition to those who argue that nuclear activities are lawful pending the entry into force of any such explicit prohibitive treaty.

Nuclear preparations also run counter to the realization of the **societal human right to development**. They 'kill' indirectly since, in the immortal words of President Eisenhower:

'Every...missile that is fired signifies in a final sense a theft from those who hunger and are not fed'.

The 1986 UN Declaration on Social Progress and Development promotes the economic benefits to the poorest countries which should flow from implementation of the duty to disarm (Art.7) (87). It also concerns itself with the qualitative dimension to development which is seen in terms of the constant improvement of the well-being of the entire population. And of course nuclear preparations strike physically and mentally, directly and indirectly, at realization of the **right to health** (88).

Dealing with the argument from State practice

What then are the strongest arguments in defence of the legality of possession?

(1) States can do whatever they are not explicitly prohibited from doing.

(2) It is customary state practice for states to possess nuclear weapons.

(3) Possession is confirmed in general conventions.

(4) The Court is unlikely to risk discrediting international law by moving so far out of line with state practice.

Defence Proposition 1:

This argument finds some support in the interwar case of the *SS Lotus* in which the Permanent Court of International Justice (PCIJ) held that 'restrictions upon the independence of states cannot be presumed'. However four years earlier, in 1923, the PCIJ had indicated that as the rules of international law developed, so too the sovereignty of states would be proportionately diminished and restricted (89).

Moreover the *Lotus* rationale was designed for the side of international law concerned with peace. It was never intended to apply to the laws of war, whose De Martens clause expressly repudiates the need for an express prohibition. Moreover the actual *Lotus* judgment, dealing with a wartime situation, failed to apply any presumption in favour of state sovereignty. (90) In any case the current ICJ would have to take account of many post-war developments.

Defence Proposition 2:

It is argued that a very wide majority of countries have implicitly concurred in nuclearism by treaty relations or otherwise.

Against this we could point to Sweden and other technologically powerful and wealthy countries which have explicitly renounced the nuclear path. Some NATO and ANZAC allies have expressed their resentment at being co-opted into nuclear defence co-operation through bases, joint exercises or port visits. Besides, the record of the UN is full of the global anti-nuclear majority urging nuclear disarmament on the nuclear countries.

However it is true to say that this defence proposition has some degree of validity. Along with arguments (3) and (4) below, it could probably sway a majority on the ICJ **if they were to be consulted on preparations tomorrow**. This does not mean that, following an anti-nuclear advisory ruling on use and threat, it will be impossible for us to turn the present 'state practice' situation around before going back to the ICJ for an Advisory Opinion on preparations.

How could this be done? The key is to remember that customary practice involves fact and meaning, i.e. state practice plus state (and other) expressions of legal obligation or legally-founded disapproval concerning the practice in question (*opinio juris*). Hitherto the anti-nuclear majority has criticised nuclear preparations mainly on political and economic grounds. But a constructive ICJ advisory opinion on use and threat could be the signal for this massive global opposition to multiply its challenges to the assumed legal status of nuclear preparations. Declaration by declaration, individually and in regional groupings and at the UN, they will be able to strip away explicitly any shreds of implicit legitimacy which could presently be argued to attach to nuclear preparations by virtue of their not having been challenged on a sufficiently consistent legal basis. Another way of establishing the necessary anti-nuclear *opinio juris* would be through a general declaratory treaty renouncing the nuclear option as already illegal and pledging co-operation for anti-nuclear law-enforcement to the point of verified global elimination.

On the other hand if *Nuremburg* and general principles of law are held to be strong enough on their own to outlaw nuclear preparations, then another general principle of law would come into play, Latin name *ex injuria non oritur jus* or 'law-breaking is not allowed to give rise to legal principles'.

'A small band of criminals never have been permitted to argue that their own lawless conduct destroys the validity of the very laws they have violated.' (91)

Moreover the nuclear powers, least of all the first such 'possessor', cannot be permitted to argue the 'exceptional necessity' of their behaviour by reference to the threat posed by the others (92). US jurist Francis Boyle has put forward the domestic-law criminal analogy of duelling, Russian Roulette or 'playing chicken' with automobiles:

'the fact that two or more individuals voluntarily participated in such a joint criminal enterprise would not excuse anyone from criminal responsibility' for *'reckless endangerment'*...The nuclear superpowers *'cannot exonerate themselves from joint and several criminal responsibility for such illegal behaviour by invoking the unlawful conduct of their co-felons'* (93).

'Necessity defences' for otherwise illegal behaviour are only open to defendants who are without blame in bringing about the exceptional circumstance in which the exceptional action was necessary (94). (An example would be breaking into someone's house to put out a fire.)

Defence Proposition 3:

The practice of the nuclear powers is supposed to have received explicit and implicit seals of approval from various conventions:

***Non-Proliferation Treaty* of 1968** (95):

This has been signed by a very large number of nations, despite a number of persistent objections to its discriminatory character. For non-nuclear countries it bans acquisition and manufacture of nuclear 'weapons' (Art.2). However Article I begins 'Each nuclear-weapon State Party' which pro-nuclear nations consider their trump card.

In reply:

(a) This would only go so far as to legitimise a totally inert possession. It does not necessarily imply legal recognition of attaching warheads to intelligence and delivery systems, let alone forward deployment;

(b) The anti-nuclear majority could argue that they had little choice but to accept *de facto* the best arrangement on offer and that the treaty was a political bargain, not one designed to alter the *de jure* situation either way (96). Indeed, if nuclear preparations were crimes against peace and humanity already in 1968, and if these crimes are considered to violate 'peremptory norms of general international law', then technically the NPT must be null and void, according to the logic of Article 53 of the *Vienna Convention on the Interpretation of Treaties* of 1969 (97) (98)

(c) Anti-nuclear countries can argue that a new situation has long been created by the nuclear nations' breach of Article 6:

'Each of the Parties...undertakes to pursue negotiations in good faith on effective measures relating to cessation of the nuclear arms race at an early date and to nuclear disarmament, and on a treaty on general and complete disarmament under strict and effective international control.'

The anti-nuclear nations are thus in a very strong position to use the 1995 Review (Extension) Conference to insist on a revision of the Treaty to reserve their position on the legal status of *de facto* possession by the nuclear nations; or else to make individual or collective declarations placing a condition on their continued adherence to the Treaty - namely that it is not to imply any *de jure* recognition of any purported customary status for these poison-scattering devices.

The *Partial Test Ban Treaty* of 1963 (99):

A similar argument can be made here to counter the claim that the partial nature of this treaty gives implicit legitimacy to underground test explosions. (Of course, the 'testing' is only testing from the point of view of a minority of the social actors affected: for the rest of us the poison is scattered for real.) All adherents to the PTB could make declarations formally opposing such a construction and deploring the failure of the nuclear nations to observe their Preamble obligations to achieve an agreement on general and complete disarmament, *'to achieve the discontinuance of all test explosions of nuclear weapons for all time'* and *'to put an end to the contamination of man's environment by radioactive substances'* (100)

Other anti-nuclear measures of local, partial and interim character:

These all need to be reviewed with the aim of registering formal diplomatic declarations. These statements would be designed to expressly negate any inference that the nuclear nations might try to draw concerning any implicit recognition of nuclear 'preparations' other than those explicitly outlawed in that treaty or measure: e.g. other than in the Latin American or South Pacific Nuclear-Free Zones; on the seabed, on the moon or in Antarctica.

Efforts to pin the nuclear nations down to more comprehensive 'negative security assurances' should avoid giving any grounds for arguing that it would be lawful to use nuclear 'weapons' against other nuclear powers, and reserve the anti-nuclear countries' position on the legal status of deployment, etc. Likewise all resolutions - and not only by governments - calling for new negotiations and treaties should either make it clear that the treaty sought would be largely *declaratory* of existing customary law, or at least reserve the anti-nuclear legal position on nuclear preparations of all kinds.

Defence Proposition 4:

This does not argue that nuclearism is lawful, simply that the ICJ might be reluctant to find them unlawful - for fear of creating a credibility gap between the world situation *de facto* and *de jure*. However:

* international law will also be brought into disrepute if it does nothing to help to close this gap;

* an initial reference on use and threat will help to lay the foundations for this gap to be tackled, especially if meanwhile, through a strategy of anti-nuclear state declarations outlined above, contesting and changing the balance of global *opinio juris*, nuclear state-practice can be denuded of any credible customary law justification.

• •

It is time to bring the era of nuclear weapons to a close. It was born out of the near breakdown of the law of war in WW2 and rationalised as a gift of God with which to hold 'the Red menace' at bay. With the ending of the Cold War the mitigating circumstances which allegedly surrounded the original descent to terrorist threats, no longer apply. We now realize that one nation's security cannot be gained at any others' expense. When the means for establishing common security are at hand humanity can no longer afford the waste, insecurity and spiritual corruption of tolerating reliance by any nation on reprisals and high-tech to do what can in any case be achieved by verified disarmament and the pacific settlement of disputes.

But the diseased cultural mentality which found expression in 'the balance of terror' will cling tenaciously to its obsessions. 'The boys' will keep on inventing appalling new 'toys'. New enemy-figures will be projected, old anxieties will be ceaselessly fanned, and new scenarios devised. Even the most comprehensive schemes for fully verified and balanced nuclear disarmament will be portrayed as vulnerable to possible circumvention by some scheming bogeyman. In appeasing the neurotic anxiety for 'total security', billions will be wasted on the sinister irrelevance of Star Wars.

That is why international lawyers should be the first to reflect on the serene and healing words of the founder of international law in the modern period, Hugo Grotius, writing in 1625:

'That the possibility of being attacked confers the right to attack is abhorrent to every principle of equity. Human life exists under such conditions that complete security is never guaranteed to us. For protection against uncertain fears we must rely on Divine Providence, and on a wariness free from reproach, not on force.' (101)

Now in the early 1990s - in addition to Divine Providence and wariness - we can look with confidence to a human institution to confirm the criminality of nuclear use and threats. Subsequently we should be prepared to return to the World Court to help us vindicate our peaceful rights against nuclear - and all other - mass-destructive preparations.

LOW-LEVEL RADIATION EFFECTS

There is no threshold level below which the effects of radiation can be dismissed as risk-free. Most victims are unaware that their ailment is connected to radiation, or can't prove that it is, owing to the deliberate underfunding of health studies to monitor health effects.

The bodies which set so-called 'safe limits' for radiation exposure and the 'acceptable risks of damage to health are largely offshoots of the nuclear industry, not the medical profession. They concentrate on the most dramatic, upsetting and politically unacceptable health effects, such as cancers, leukaemia and gross genetic malformations. They also concentrate on short-term consequences, ignoring the sheer longevity of many of the radionucleides arising in the nuclear industry and from nuclear weapon activities.

Studies of Hiroshima/Nagasaki victims conceived after the atomic explosions have failed to show increased chromosomal abnormality in subsequent live-births. However:

* a selected non-average population received this radiation, the so-called 'healthy survivor' effect;
* genetic effects may only appear if the radiation doses are low enough for the cells to retain their normal reproductive activity;
* children who survived are only now reaching the age when many cancers become manifest - many more than expected could develop in the next few years;
* the effects of recessive mutations are only likely to become apparent over many generations;

'A mild mutation may express itself in humans as an allergy, asthma, juvenile diabetes, hypertension, arthritis, high blood cholesterol level, slight muscular or bone defects...These defects in genetic make-up leave the individual slightly less able to cope with ordinary stresses and hazards in the environment. Increasing the number of such genetic 'mistakes' in a family line, each passed on to the next generation, while at the same time increasing the stresses and hazards in the environment, leads to termination of the family line through infertility and/or death prior to reproductive age. On a large scale, such a process leads to selective genocide or species suicide.' (102)

Even calculating only until the year 2000, Dr Bertell estimates between half and nine million children genetically damaged as a result of the production and testing of nuclear weapons since 1945. The UN Scientific Committee on the Effects of Atomic Radiation has calculated 43,000 expressed genetic defects by the year 2000 from atmospheric testing (ibid, p.105). (103)

Part Four: Potentials of the UN System

Security Council, United Nations, New York

Photo: UN Chen/jr

10. Approaching the ICJ

When addressing such a momentous issue it is desirable that the World Court should feel that it has the trust and encouragement of the great majority of the world community. Although telegrams of support from NGOs might fortify its confidence at the right time, there can be no substitute for a resounding vote of confidence from the UN General Assembly itself (or other requesting body, see later). Technically a slim majority in the GA could push a reference through as a 'non-important question'. Since it obviously is an 'important question' (for which a two-thirds GA majority is needed), this would send all the wrong signals to the world and to the ICJ.

To help ensure a large majority it is desirable that the resolutions moving reference to the World Court be **brought by a group of countries** with different legal codes, ideologies and religions; rich and poor, 'capitalist' and 'socialist'; with foreign policies which are aligned, non-aligned and neutral. Considering that several of the nuclear nations can be expected to use their economic and political clout to punish anti-nuclear 'troublemakers' (especially small isolated ones) the chances of persuading a substantial group of nations to bring an Article 96 reference are probably much better than the chance of persuading a single country to do so on its own.

Moreover, a broad spread of movers and supporters will be crucial for disarming politically-motivated criticism within and by the nuclear weapon states whose ruling elites will doubtless try to argue along the following lines:

> Such a reference would be 'political as opposed to legal', and 'an abuse of judicial process'. It would lead to the ICJ 'discrediting the cause of the rule of international law' by 'trying to do too much', encroaching on 'particularly sensitive' issues which are to do with ultimate power and (allegedly) reserved to the sovereign discretion of individual nation States. If the Court were to give an opinion on such 'inherently non-justiciable subject-matter', it would be proving that it had 'gone political' and was no longer worthy of respect (1).

This portrayal of the issue as primarily political and such a prescriptive view of the correct role of the Court are themselves highly political! (2) Since Article 65 of the Court Statue reads:

'The Court may [NB - not 'shall'] give an advisory opinion on any legal question...'

Nations who think along these lines should be invited to argue their cases before the Court itself.

It is true, however, that one reason why the Court might try to reject such a request would be if it felt that whatever it said would be ignored. The Court will prefer to be asked questions which do not require it to move too far ahead of 'political realities', including UN resolutions and public opinion. Since it will take time for the leaders and publics of the nuclear states to give up their nuclear addictions, more than one reference - and a lot of follow up activities in between - will probably be necessary and desirable from several points of view.

The scope of the question

These various inter-related aspects are brilliantly analysed in Erich Geiringer's discussion paper, *Courting the Question*, recently published as part of a series by the New Zealand section of IPPNW. Extracts follow:

'The World Court Project will have to decide what to ask the Court, bearing in mind that the question:

* *must be acceptable to a majority of the chosen Organ of the UN;*
* *must be deemed appropriate by the Court;*
* *should give minimal toe-hold to the opposition;*
* *and should, whatever the outcome, advance and not hinder the anti-nuclear cause.'*

The anti-nuclear mindset

In the face of an unprecedented threat to the survival of human civilisation... our largely unofficial, minority protest movement...has inevitably developed certain quasi-religious traits.

Righteousness sustains the soul but it is not good brain food. The need to convince can become an urge to convert, drive becomes zeal. This mindset is an obstacle in addressing interim objectives when pragmatism, restraint and precision are required.

Having failed to nip nuclearism in the bud, we have to work within the nuclear realities which have since unfolded. To succeed in the elimination of nuclear weapons we must be prepared to proceed with due regard to what can be realistically achieved at each stage.

The Court

When discussing the World Court Project, pessimists have warned us that 'We are bound to lose', 'It's a bad Court', 'It is all political', 'It is not a judicial agency but a tool of the nuclear powers'. On the other hand enthusiasts see the Court as a chance to loosen every available argument in the anti-nuclear quiver and to march off victoriously with nuclearism writhing in the dust. These extremes won't serve. We must proceed on certain sane assumptions:

The Court does not frame laws. Attempts to make it do will fail to get our questions to the Court or give the Court and opposing lawyers the chance to evade the issues. We must not confuse the activity of asking the ICJ for an advisory opinion with the activity of formulating anti-nuclear laws.

The Court is not infallible. The easier we make it for the Court the less likely is it to fail us. Multiple and complex questions provide opportunities for the Court to evade us, the opposition to spike us, and for us to trip over our own feet.

The Court does not function in a rarefied academic atmosphere. It will hesitate to give an opinion which is irreconcilable with political reality. We should not put the Court into a position where it must either dilute [its] judgement...or put America on more of a collision course with the UN than it is already. We want the USA to beat an orderly retreat. It would be counter-productive to drive America into explicit opposition to declared international law. The Court's opinion need not please the USA, but it should give her time to accommodate.

The Preparatory Phase

Some people think that we should make the most of our day in Court and obtain opinions on every kind of question to do with nuclearism. This would be quite impractical. If such a questionnaire ever got before the Court, obfuscation, red herrings, delays, ancient precedents and modern instances would entangle us in a web of our own weaving. We would invite exactly the kind of negative or inconclusive opinion which our meticulousness was designed to prevent. The USA is no longer in a position to make a frontal attack on the anti-nuclear case. A questionnaire would offer an opportunity to harass our flanks and rear sufficiently to frustrate our main purpose of inducing the Court to send a clear signal around the world.

Fortunately, we would never get past the lobbying stage with such a questionnaire. International reality will take over as soon as we try to get a UN Organ to pop the question. There will be determined efforts, from without and within the UN, to persuade and pressurise the Organs not to go to Court.

The nuclear powers do not wish to appear in the spotlight of an ICJ hearing but they will hide this simple fact behind arguments of a complex political, economic, and military nature, carefully tailored to the interests and sensitivities of the target nation they are lobbying. It will be then that we shall appreciate the virtue of the simple question which everybody can live with, which gives no opening to the machinations of the counter-lobby and which yet serves our purpose.

Keeping the question simple...will provide the nuclear powers with fewer blackmail points. For example, questioning activities such as manufacture, storage, transport, and deployment could easily frighten countries which manufacture components or sell uranium, host ships or take part in joint exercises. The use question offers none of these pressure points and would make it difficult for the opposition to gain the votes of non-nuclear countries.

Should our lobbying chip away patiently so that we can promote a really comprehensive reference, which will do the job properly once and for all? Unfortunately, this won't work. Slow lobbying becomes a labour of Sisyphus due to the turn-over of diplomats and administrations and the much longer time it would take to conduct discussions at the UN and with sending governments about drafting and co-sponsoring a resolution with a wide scope. The volatile world situation makes legal challenge a matter of urgency.

What to ask

If we accept that the question should be simple, we shall be driven irresistibly to the one question without which the others cannot be decided and from which the answers to all the other questions will flow in time: the question of use.

We want the Court to advise the world whether nuclear weapons may be used or whether they belong to a category such as that to which biological weapons have already been consigned. If their use is forbidden, a basis for progress towards eventual total nuclear disarmament is created, but until their illegality is clearly established this prospect will slip further and further into wishful thinking.

Opting for the simple question of use will expedite preparation and lobbying, will stymie the opposition and would serve us well in the event of defeat because the whole world would very clearly understand what had been denied. It is unlikely that either the Court or America would want to live with the consequences of such an understanding. The Court would lose status, which is all it has to lose, but America would destroy its chances of creating a new world order if she were seen to argue [openly and publicly] for the use of nuclear weapons.

What not to ask

If use is forbidden all the other modalities can be made to wither away under conventions, UN resolutions, Security Council actions, domestic enactments, etc [though one or two additional references to the Court may still be needed to give the necessary jolts KM]. But until use is forbidden none of this will happen for lack of the necessary logical, legal, and even moral basis to make it happen.

Testing

We have invested so much effort over the years in trying to stop nuclear tests that some will want to put this question before the Court. We are reluctant to face up to the counter-productive weaknesses of a test ban campaign in the absence of a legal prohibition on use. The test ban campaign has however had valuable educational spin-offs. We were also seduced by the false dawn of the Partial Test Ban Treaty which we extrapolated into a hope for the 'next step'.

The PTBT, while of great value to the environment, did not slow the nuclear arms race, nor reduce the danger of nuclear warfare. On the contrary, it enabled the nuclear powers to pursue their madness underground, without having to deal with the public indignation aroused by the less efficient atmospheric tests.

The nuclear powers, and the USA in particular, will not stop testing in the absence of clearly phased-in and supervised total nuclear disarmament....They will, no doubt, obligingly, reduce underground tests to the degree to which they can successfully replace them by new laboratory and computer methodology.

...Asking the ICJ a question about testing would be confusing and irrelevant to the point of mischief. Just imagine if the Court dithered on use and covered up its dithering by coming out strongly against underground tests.

First Use

Any attempt to outlaw 'First use' is tantamount to silent legitimisation of 'second use', i.e. of nuclear retaliation. That, of course, legitimises the doctrine of nuclear deterrence. We have witnessed over the years the inevitable dynamic consequences of basing security on this doctrine.

To single out 'First use' for special prohibition means that if a country were to devastate another, with all the dire effects for the rest of the world, it would be legitimate for the surviving nuclear defences of that country in turn, to double or treble that devastation, without regard to the damage to our biosphere.

Emphasising the difference between first use and subsequent uses would merely encourage the time honoured trick of camouflaging surprise attacks by faking a first use provocation.

For genuine progress towards a nuclear free world we should shun the 'First use' issue like a plague.

Arguments against posing the Use question

The argument has been advanced that the illegality of the use of nuclear weapons is now a settled issue and that 'in all practical, foreseeable circumstances such a use would be illegal'. To go to Court would therefore be to spend time and energy in order to risk losing what we already have. This seems another instance of paranoia in supposing that the ICJ would overturn a 'settled' rule in international law.

While it may be true that any user of nukes would be found guilty of a crime against humanity, provided he and his cronies lost the war, our task is to prevent such an eventuality. To achieve this, an opinion from the ICJ would be a valuable addition to the above cited 'legal certainty'. As there are large sections of political opinion, which still produce arguments to support the legality of nuclear weapons and even continue to vote for the right to first use in the UN, the notion of the issue being settled is, for practical purposes, false.

Lawyers who believe that the argument about use is to all intents and purposes settled are inclined to argue that if we do go to Court we should ask it to settle other questions, such as the legality of manufacture, possession, etc, and this would lead us into the quagmire described above.

Though only an ingredient, a declaration by the ICJ that the use of nuclear weapons is forbidden is essential to the process of overcoming the nuclear danger. Laws must be affirmed before they can be enforced; and the means of enforcement will avail nothing in the absence of the will to use them.

Throughout its history, a majority of the UN has consistently indicated the will to adopt an anti-nuclear regime and, given the means, would no doubt be willing to enforce it. There is now a chance that the need to prevent horizontal proliferation might bring Washington to the party. An ICJ opinion could help steer the USA towards this desirable conclusion when the law, the force, and the will are finally brought together.

• •

Of course the menace of nuclear 'weapons' will not really be overcome until all these poison-scattering devices are eliminated world-wide - and indeed all other indiscriminate engines, strategies and tactics of mass destruction. That must be the essential long-term aim of the World Court Project. But the above analysis convinces us that we may approach this goal faster if we take two or more steps, rather than attempt a single, huge and risky leap.

It goes without saying that each step should open the way for the next one(s) and not make future progress more difficult. Since there is a danger of the nuclear weapon states seeking to draw conclusions claiming to legitimise nuclear possession if we take the more limited initial option, the wording of the preamble to any reference resolution should guard against this by referring to nuclear evils other than those which flow from use and threat. For the same reason the operative sentence should also keep the door open for further questions - see draft resolution put forward by WCP-UK.

Which organ should ask the court?

Much depends on our frame of reference. If we insist on seeing it from our own point of view as citizens of the planet endowed with inalienable human rights and concern for the ecological integrity of our earth, then for us it seems logical that the General Assembly [GA] is not necessarily the only body we should try to work through.

On the other hand the nuclear powers are wedded to the preconception that nukes are normal 'weapons', hence their particular business, an affair between governments, especially between 'responsible' nuclear-possessing governments. Or else they may consider nukes a serious criminal matter for the Security Council if certain uncontrollable newcomers are seeking to break into the nuclear club, eg Iraq, Pakistan, North Korea, or 'terrorists'.

Either way, they will consider it quite inappropriate to have other UN bodies moving into their special preserve of the maintenance of international peace and security.

Several UN bodies have the right to make advisory references. They include the FAO, UNESCO, the IAEA, and the Trusteeship Council (which is empowered to receive petitions). There would be no shortage of things which these bodies could do in support of an advisory opinion strategy, but it is realistic to limit discussion to just three bodies as the main potential askers: the Economic and Social Council (ECOSOC), and the Assembly of the World Health Organisation (WHO), and the General Assembly itself.

ECOSOC

The Council is composed of 54 members elected by the GA for three year terms. It meets twice a year, in New York and Geneva, and has majority voting. In theory therefore only 28 nations could authorize an ICJ-reference, as opposed to the 100-115 or so needed through the GA (two thirds of members present and voting). This would certainly make lobbying ECOSOC a lot easier and also discussions to agree on the text of a resolution. However in order to fortify the confidence of the ICJ, we should aim for an over two-thirds majority in whatever forum we are working through. And ease of lobbying is only one criterion. Other factors, such as moral authority may point to sending the issue to the ICJ with well over 100 nations in support, even though this will take more time and work.

Working under the authority of the GA, ECOSOC promotes progress across a wide field of responsibilities:

a) conditions of economic and social progress and development;
b) solutions of international economic, social, health, and related problems...
c) universal respect for, and observance of, human rights and fundamental freedoms (UN Charter, Art.55)

'All Members pledge themselves to take joint and separate action in co-operation with the Organization for the achievement of the [above] purposes.' (Art.56)

ECOSOC may make or initiate studies and can make recommendations concerning the above areas. It can prepare draft conventions, call conferences, co-ordinate the activities of specialized agencies and furnish information to the SC.(Arts.62,63) It is clear that it could play an active part in leading up to and supporting any advisory request by the GA or WHO.

If ECOSOC asks its own question, or endorses the request of another UN body, the question would have to be one 'arising within the scope of its activities' (Art.96.2) Disagreements within ECOSOC on whether to accept a strongly anti-nuclear report from ECOSOC's Human Rights Commission, WHO or the ILC could provide the peg for an ICJ advisory reference.

Apart from its special concern for human rights and development the other main reason to favour working through ECOSOC is its permeability to citizens groups. It consults with international non-governmental organisations (NGOs) 'which are concerned with matters within its competence', and with such national NGOs as that state member does not object to (Art.71).

NGO REGISTER

The Yearbook of International Organisations reprints the NGO Register which is divided into three categories.

* Category III (The Roster) - about 600 organisations make occasional contributions to ECOSOC but may have a closer relationship with some other body;
* Category II - about 350 organisations have a specific competence in ECOSOC activities, and are also granted hearings. They include IPB, Greenpeace International, Friends of the Earth, Friends World Committee for Consultation, the International Commission of Health Professionals for Health and Human Rights, many voluntary, religious, professional, ethnic and women's organisations and others representing the young, the old, the disabled and so forth.
* Category I - about 40 organisations are involved in most activities of ECOSOC and can propose agenda items. They include international organisations of Parliamentarians, Labour Unions, Local Authorities, Co-operatives, Religious groupings, Women, Youth, War Veterans, the League of Red Cross and Crescent Societies and the World Federation of United Nations Associations.

The Congress of Organisations with Consultative Status with ECOSOC (CONGO) brings together a wide range of such bodies.

These arrangements make ECOSOC an attractive focus for lobbying. WCP-activists will be able to involve many of these citizens groups by consulting and encouraging them to take full advantage of their opportunities for influencing this part of the UN system. The 54 national delegations would find themselves approached through existing channels and known contacts.

World Health Organisation

WHO has an Executive Board of 31 'expert' members who serve in a personal capacity, not as government representatives. In 1991 23 were from the South, only five from Western European and 'other'. Half are voted in by each annual World Health Assembly (WHA) open to all UN members and held in Geneva, where some NGOs have offices which could support a systematic lobby. It also has a developed structure of six regional committees where pressure could be built up, and regional offices in Brazzaville, Washington, Alexandria, Copenhagen, New Delhi and Manila.

The expert members of WHO will hopefully be somewhat independent of the pressures of their own Foreign Ministries. WHO executive members, WHA delegates and national Health Ministries would be especially ready to listen to organisations of health professionals who lobby them and with whom WHO can 'consult and co-operate on matters within its competence' (WHO Constitution, Art.71 = W.71). There is an obvious co-ordinating role here for IPPNW, which has indeed already begun.

Disputes about the interpretation or application of WHO's constitution 'shall be referred to the ICJ' (W.75). In a separate Agreement between the UN and WHO the latter is authorized to request advisory opinions of the ICJ 'on legal questions arising within the scope of its competence.' (Art.X,2). There might be argument about this, but certainly WHO's Objective and Functions are drawn very widely.

The Objective is 'the attainment by all peoples of the highest possible level of health' (W.1), defined in the preamble as 'complete physical, mental and social wellbeing and not merely the absence of disease' and affirmed as a 'basic human right'. Any approach to the ICJ from WHO would seem to have an excellent chance in view of:

* the assault on health and on medical facilities which nuclear war would inevitably involve (Use);
* the 'nuclear numbing', mental stress and spiritual anguish inflicted by the nuclear powers 'even before the bomb drops' (3) ('Deterrence').

Moreover in due course even possession could be shown as detrimental to WHO's Global Strategy for Health for All by the Year 2000 in the light of:

* the damage now being inflicted on expectant mothers, the unborn and future generations
* what scientists now know about the impossibility of eliminating the risk of accidental detonations, or even of war - although of course it will be open to the nuclear powers to argue before the ICJ that only their deterrent preparedness has fended off the worse health-dangers of nuclear war!

WHO's Functions include 'being the directing authority on international health work' and 'generally to take all action necessary to attain the objective' (W.2a and v); more specifically health education, preventive, environmental and mental health work are all authorized as well as 'assist[ing] in developing an informed public opinion among all peoples on matters of health' (W.2r) WHO has already done work on nuclear winter (4) and radiation damage which echoes the IPPNW motto: Prevention is the only cure for nuclear war.

IPPNW (International Physicians for the Prevention of Nuclear War) has had official relations at the international level with WHO since 1985, and several affiliates have good connections with its regional offices. Furthermore IPPNW collaborated on the 1984/87 WHO study 'Effects of Nuclear War on Health and Health Services' and WHO spokespersons have addressed IPPNW congresses. There is also a precedent for WHO approaching the ICJ: in 1980 WHO requested 'an interpretation of the agreement of 25 March 1951 between the WHO and Egypt.' These positive indications seemed to be bearing some fruit when - as this text went to press - news was received that the resolution (urging an ICJ reference) to be put forward by Colombia at Committee B of the World Health Assembly in May 1992 was likely to be supported by 'many delegates'. These include some of the CIS states and in particular the Malaysian Minister of Health, who has indicated his intention of raising the Colombian initiative at the Commonwealth of Nations meeting just before the WHA.

Dr Erich Geiringer, IPPNW, New Zealand

THE COMMON DUTY OF MEDICINE AND LAW

In 1984 the Medical-Juridical Committee of the Commune of Venice organised a conference on the incompatibility of Italy's constitution with the introduction of American Cruise missiles. The conference declared that:

'Medicine and Law share a common, indefeasible duty: to defend life, health and human society....Medicine is not encroaching on others' preserves when it studies and resorts to legal instruments, where these instruments are apt to prevent disease: indeed it is part of the physician's duty.'

General Assembly

There are also strong arguments for mounting our main lobbying effort towards the GA. The powers of the GA will be dealt with in the next chapter, here we will simply suggest that the GA may be the best place to make the first reference on Use/Threat, for the following reasons:

* The sheer weight of the issue warrants it being discussed in the full world arena, one where the menace to world security and alternatives to 'Peace Through Terror' can be considered along with the health and human rights dimensions.
* This would be expected by most Non-Aligned diplomats, not just those of the nuclear powers and the Security Council.
* A reference having the scope of Use/Threat will echo the resolutions brought to the GA over many years by India and passed overwhelmingly by this body.
* A reference from the GA would gain most publicity and help to ensure that enough countries and organisations would be committed to following through on the implications of the advisory response when it came after a year or two.

However once the interest of the world has been roused by the sending of an initial advisory request on Use/Threat, and even more by the contents of the reply, it could be preferable for any follow-up advisory request on Preparations to come from WHO and/or ECOSOC. This shift could itself mark a shift away from an understanding of nuclearism based on purely military considerations to one focusing more on the long-range effects of radioactivity.

In any case it is wise for us to work with the grain of the specialist abilities and existing contacts of those organisations who become committed to this Project. It may be that lobbying through ECOSOC or WHO do not initially succeed in getting those organisations to send a reference to the ICJ, but they could have very useful next-best outcomes:

* sending strong recommendations to the GA - and even the Security Council! - asking them to consider a reference request;
* associating themselves formally with a GA Advisory Opinion in the months after it has been requested; or
* putting particular effort into responding to the request of the ICJ for written submissions relevant to the issue which the GA had laid

before it, including these bodies conveying to the Hague the written submissions of NGOs in consultative status with them along with any petitions and Declarations of the Public Conscience which they may have received.

In this way we will advance over a broad front and accumulate moral and political pressure in depth. Nobody can tell how quickly and in which UN organ we will make a breakthrough. The World Court Project is still very much in evolution and in any case the actual outcome will probably flow from various sources and factors, only some of which citizens' groups will be able to influence.

Perhaps the biggest problem we shall face is the threat of the nuclear powers and their allies cutting off funding to countries which 'cause trouble' or agencies which 'go political', including the UN as a whole (to give this threat teeth the biggest contributor to the UN likes to keep $3-400 million dollars in arrears). For this reason it is vital that contingency plans are prepared, and committed anti-nuclear nations who can afford to, be encouraged to create contingency solidarity funds, such as a percentage of oil exports. A small tax, properly promoted and 'sold' to a nation's citizens could be a way of educating them about the ICJ-case and giving them a good feeling of contributing to a world-wide campaign for a safer world for all. While recognising the continuing urgency of the nuclear peril and the power of the nuclear club, we should never underestimate the wellsprings of goodwill, solidarity and creativity which this strategy could draw out in ordinary people worldwide, as we begin to glimpse light at last at the end of the nuclear tunnel!

Footnote:

As this text was going to press it was announced that the Colombian delegation has put forward a resolution giving notice of their intention to propose a supplementary item to be added to the agenda of Committee B at the May 1992 World Health Assembly. The content of the item is a proposal for the WHA to request an Advisory Opinion from the World Court on the legal status of nuclear weapons. Whether this proposal will eventually reach the floor of the WHA is impossible to predict with certainty, but it represents a very encouraging first step within the UN system towards the eventual attainment of our goal.

11. After the ICJ responds

In this chapter we assume that the ICJ has responded in a reasonably united manner and that this response condemns as illegal the use and threat of nuclear 'weapons'. Of course other outcomes are conceivable, including a badly split decision or different verdicts on threat as distinct from use. In this case we will need to redouble our efforts to accumulate national, international and other declarations in order to tip the scales of legal opinion against nuclearism. **Precedent exists for such declarations to lead the ICJ to change its mind**, when coupled with the adverse reaction of world opinion and changes in membership of the Court:

'The inspired judicial dissenting opinion of today that seeks to develop the positive law dialectically in accord with changing history is so often the judicial orthodoxy of tomorrow or the day after tomorrow. Within five years of the South West Africa, Second Phase, single-vote-majority ruling [effectively permitting the continuation of Apartheid - KM], the International Court was given a second chance on the same issue. By lop-sided, 13-to-2 and 11-to-4 votes on the substantive legal issues, the Court proceeded essentially to reverse the 1966 ruling, in the 1971 Advisory Opinion in Namibia.' (5)

Repercussions within national legal and political systems

A fairly united and clear advisory response condemning nuclear use and threat will have important repercussions around the world:

* In nuclear nations public opinion can be expected to swing in favour of a more serious approach to nuclear disarmament negotiations.

* Several countries currently allied with nuclear nations are likely to break ranks diplomatically and to oppose the extension or continuation of various forms of nuclear co-operation.

* Anti-nuclear countries and activists will seek to use this initial Advisory Opinion as a stepping-stone towards the only really secure 'negative security assurance', namely the verified worldwide elimination of all nuclear warheads and associated facilities and systems.

Besides the political effects stemming from the clarification of the existing illegality of nuclear use and threat, there will also be major legal consequences. Many countries have national constitutions which directly incorporate international law into the domestic legal system:

* The Constitution of the USA provides that international treaties shall be part of 'the supreme law of the land' (Art. VI,2) ;
* In the UK the traditional rule has been that 'the [customary] law of nations in its fullest extent is and forms part of the law of England'. (6)

When peace activists in these countries have sought to rely on these constitutional fundamentals, the courts have been able to take refuge in the allegedly vague and disputed character of international law - one escape route which a firm and clear Advisory Opinion will close in the future.

The military manuals of these and other nuclear nations claim to respect international law and urge military personnel to disobey 'manifestly unlawful commands' (7). Once a resolute Advisory Opinion makes it clear that any nuclear use would be criminal, how will top commanders and superior officers be able to issue and transmit orders to use nuclear 'weapons' even in rehearsals without a degree of risk of themselves being arrested? In this way an unravelling of nuclear 'deterrorism' could come about, with a form of 'internal legal self-deterrence' complementing external factors such as fear of world reaction, nuclear retaliation, and boomeranging environmental damage (8).

A similar close relationship exists between international and domestic law in other Western countries, e.g. Netherlands and Germany, both of whom have seen legally-aware movements of nuclear refusal emerge in their armed forces. After World War 2 the Allies forced the three Axis powers to accept constitutions which bound them internally to operate within the constraints of international law. An Advisory Opinion by the World Court can be expected to lead to greatly increased legal and political pressure on all these governments to observe their own constitutional constraints and to break all ties with nuclear terrorism. The potential for the mobilisation of popular pressure on this kind of legal issue has been seen clearly in the constitutional debate in Germany and Japan during and after the Gulf War.

New opinions in international relations

Many other nations have constitutions which oblige their rulers to respect and/or promote international law, e.g. India. This internal obligation is additional to the external obligation as a member of the family of nations to respect the law of nations. An anti-nuclear Advisory Opinion on use/threat will encourage individual foreign ministries and regional groupings and agencies to review their past diplomatic record, some or much of which was probably shaped under the apathy-inducing suspicion that nothing they did or said would make much difference to the nuclear powers. Once the ICJ emerges on the horizon as a powerful moral and legal ally, anti-nuclear countries may feel spurred to correct any previous collaboration by issuing appropriate diplomatic declarations, protests and counter-reservations.

Another option which will open up is for countries to consider individual or collective attempts to take all or some of the nuclear nations to the World Court in a contentious case or series of linked proceedings. Such a move would require careful preparation and much deliberation. Considering the reluctance of the nuclear nations to accept the compulsory jurisdiction of the ICJ, considerable research would be needed to identify the necessary treaties from which the ICJ could establish its legal competence to assume jurisdiction, hear the case and then issue a binding ruling. Naturally anti-nuclear countries may be reluctant to pursue the nuclear nations through the Court for non-legal reasons, e.g. big power disapproval, sanctions and so on. But it seems doubtful that the problem of establishing jurisdiction would prove insurmountable, given the vast web of treaty-relations stemming from a whole range of multilateral and bilateral agreements. To take an example: the 1965 *Treaty for Conciliation, Judicial Settlement* and *Arbitration between the UK and the Swiss Confederation* provides for either party to insist on judicial settlement by the ICJ if conciliation fails (9).

A GENERAL TREATY FOR GLOBAL ABOLITION?

Other than the political pressures of the powerful nuclear nations, there is nothing legally to stop a few leading anti-nuclear nations or a single regional grouping from concluding a *'General Treaty for the Elimination of All 'Weapons of Mass Destruction'* and then working for wider and wider accessions, eventually including the nuclear nations themselves.

In the treaty the parties could:

* constitute a *League of Anti-Nuclear Nations* founded on their understanding of the existing criminality of nuclear preparations of any kind anywhere;
* place this understanding as a condition for their continued adherence to all measures of partial or local nuclear disarmament (e.g. Partial Test Ban Treaty, NPT, Treaties of Tlatelolco or Raratonga, pursuit of interim security assurances from the nuclear powers;
* agree to work together and through groupings such as the Non-Aligned Movement, for another anti-nuclear reference to the ICJ (on preparations and possession), or possibly for a collective contentious case aiming for a binding judgment;
* append detailed Compliance Schedules and Verification Regimes - or guidelines for their creation and updating - which would come into force when a sufficient number of countries had ratified the corresponding sections of the General Treaty (i.e. those concerning Use, Testing and Research, Manufacture and Uranium Enrichment, Deployment, Uncoupling and Dismantling of Warheads).

The idea of, for example, Costa Rica, Mexico, Nigeria and Egypt signing such a treaty may seem pointless, but only to those who have not grasped the fundamental, exciting truth: Although there is nothing which four - or even 160 - anti-nuclear powers can do to force the nuclear powers to respect the rule of law, there is nothing in law which the nuclear minority can do to prevent the anti-nuclear nations and NGOs stripping away any last vestiges of legal acceptability from things nuclear. The very 'powerlessness' of such a diplomatic offensive would underline and boldly celebrate this other kind of power - on the plane of moral and legal meaning - whose accumulation is the necessary precondition for progress on the physical plane.

Potentials of the UN system

In what follows we concentrate on how the anti-nuclear global majority could work through the UN to capitalize on a favourable ICJ Advisory Opinion. Given the scope for abuse inherent in the prominent role of the Security Council (SC) with its built-in privileges for five nuclear powers, the global anti-nuclear majority is faced with an obvious problem. The same problem confronts the many excellent proposals for UN reform (10), since Article 108 allows a single permanent member of the SC to veto any amendment to the Charter.

Major changes in national constitutions do not usually stem from an abstract concern for formal constitution innovation. They usually originate from impasse between powerful groupings engaged in struggle over vital issues affecting ordinary citizens (see current developments in Eastern Europe or South Africa). If one or more ICJ-references can be used to jolt the nuclear nations into serious nuclear disarmament, this could be the icebreaker for more general moves to reform the UN system.

At all events what follows will focus on the scope for useful moves within the UN as it is at present, always remembering:

* The nuclear powers cannot be disarmed against their will. Just like ICJ-opinions themselves, all the preceding and follow-up activities, resolutions, study groups, special commissions, etc will be aiming to focus world concern, and accumulate more and more moral and legal legitimacy towards the elimination of all weapons of mass destruction. This is somewhat like the 'positional play' of a chess expert who slowly reduces the opponent's scope for manoeuvre.
* The nuclear powers dispose of enormous resources with which to pressurise not just small and poor, but even quite large, wealthy countries. They can manipulate world opinion, use covert action tactics, raise distracting scares and bogeymen, and so on (11).

Anti-nuclear governments and their supporters will need all the integrity, determination and solidarity they can muster!

Role of the General Assembly

What the nuclear nations do not have is numbers. Conventional wisdom depicts the GA as 'just a talking-shop'. But if its recommendations have not been acted on this is not the fault of the countries of the South; often it is because the rich and/or nuclear powers have chosen to block sensible recommendations and to circumvent the UN through other agencies, e.g. control of the IMF, World Bank, etc through the G7 club.

Contrary to many assumptions the constitutional position of the Security Council is not unassailable. On receiving an initial anti-nuclear Advisory Opinion the GA would have many options and latent powers. A close reading of the Charter shows that if the global anti-nuclear majority were ever to attain the necessary unity and resolution, the constitutional ways and means exist for the GA and ICJ together to prevail over the nuclear-weapon-State dominated Security Council.

1) The GA has to consider and **approve the UN budget** (C.17).- which could be important in a prolonged tussle with the SC.

2) The GA can **initiate studies** for the progressive development of international law (C.13.a)- usually through its Sixth (legal) Committee or through the authoritative International Law Commission (which works rather slowly however, only meeting once a year in Geneva). It can also initiate other studies concerning health, human rights, etc which will usually be carried out under the auspices of the relevant specialised agency.

3) 'The GA may **establish such subsidiary organs** as it deems necessary for the performance of its functions.' (C.22) One such is the Scientific Committee on Atomic Radiation (UNSCEAR), another is the Disarmament Commission, which meets in New York every May.

4) The GA can ask the Secretary-General (S-G) to **convene such special sessions** as it may require (C.20) and **discuss draft conventions** submitted to it by ECOSOC (C.62.3) or some other body. These can result in UN Conventions or unanimous or near-unanimous resolutions of the UN - activities which are legislative or 'quasi-legislative' (Falk). (12)

5) The GA can make **additional advisory requests** to the ICJ when the time is ripe in the light of:

* the content of the initial reference obtained

* the lack of heed paid to it by nuclear and would-be nuclear powers

* subsequent diplomatic developments, UN resolutions, declarations by governments and NGOs, and reports by specialized agencies and study groups.

6) The GA can also **refer issues to other UN bodies.** It could also enlist ECOSOC, WHO and other UN bodies in the follow-up to an initial ICJ-reference about nuclear use. Both bodies could be asked for their views by the GA and could reply recommending a subsequent reference on Preparations. If the GA asked the follow-up question they could formally associate themselves with the reference, and in any case would be asked by the ICJ for their views.

7) The GA **chooses the ten members of the SC** due regard being paid to their contribution to 'the maintenance of international peace and security and to the other purposes of the Organization, and also to equitable geographical distribution' (C.23.1) The current formula is 5 from African and Asian states, 1 from Eastern European states, 2 from Latin-American states (includes the Caribbean) and 2 from Western European and other states (13).

8) The GA may **discuss any questions** or any matters within the scope of the present Charter or relating to the powers and functions of any organs provided for in the present Charter...' (C.10) including 'the general principles of co-operation in the maintenance of international peace and security [and] the principles governing disarmament' (C.11.1) and more specific 'questions relating to the maintenance of international peace and security brought before it' by any state (C.11.2).

9) The GA may **call the attention** of the SC to situations likely to endanger world security (C.11.3).

10) The GA may **make recommendations** on any of these questions to the members, the Security Council or both (C.10,11) And

'Subject to the provisions of Article 12 [see below], the General Assembly may recommend measures for the peaceful adjustment of any situation, regardless of origin, which it deems likely to impair the general welfare...,.including situations resulting from a violation of the provisions of the present Charter setting forth the Purposes and Principles of the UN.' (C.14)

However:

* if action is necessary on a question relating to world peace, the GA is supposed to refer the matter to the SC (C.11); and
* the SC has first claim to deal with all matters relating to world peace:

'While the SC is exercising in respect of any dispute or situation the functions assigned to it in the present Charter, the GA shall not make any recommendation with regard to that dispute or situation unless the SC so requests.' (C.12.1)

But supposing that, emboldened by the advice of the ICJ and angered by the way the nuclear club were ignoring it, the GA was to argue that by its inaction or actions the SC was either not exercising its Charter powers or breaching the Charter? Precedent exists for the GA to recommend powerful action on the basis that it has a residual responsibility for the maintenance of world security, namely the 'Uniting for Peace' resolution it passed on 3rd November 1950 recommending armed police action in Korea. Admittedly, this had been at the request of the Security Council, fearful that the Soviet Union would veto further involvement when it stopped boycotting the meetings of the SC. But the reasoning which deduced a secondary responsibility for peace located in the GA was approved by the ICJ in Certain Expenses of the UN (14)

General Assembley begins Special Session on Disarmament, May 1978.
Photo: UN/Saw Lwin

The role of the Security Council - Possibilities for action

Voting.

The ten non-permanent members serve for two-year terms. All fifteen members have a vote and decisions have to be made 'on an affirmative vote of nine members'. In the case of non-procedural matters, decisions require the 'concurring votes of the permanent members'. As in the vote for 'necessary action' against Iraq, when China abstained, the SC has tended to rewrite this as if it said 'with no permanent member voting against'.

In order to promote world peace 'with the least diversion for armaments of the world's human and economic resources, the SC shall be responsible for formulating, with the assistance of the Military Staff Committee referred to in Article 47, plans to be submitted to the Members of the UN for the establishment of a system for the regulation of armaments'. (C.26) The MSC has hitherto remained a virtual dead letter but it is supposed to consist of the Chiefs of Staff of the permanent members. In other words, the ***UN Charter requires the nuclear powers to be pro-active*** concerning nuclear armaments, the arms trade, etc and not to drag their feet.

The Security Council has powers to monitor serious disputes (C.34), make procedural suggestions (C.36.1) and, 'if the parties fail to settle it by the means indicated in Article 33', the SC can recommend 'such terms of settlement as it may consider appropriate' (C.37). However:

* *'the SC should ...take into consideration that legal disputes should as a general rule be referred by the parties to the ICJ.'* (C.36.3); moreover:
* *'a party to a dispute shall abstain from voting'* on the SC (C.27.3). This could in theory be one way round the veto problem, so long as nine SC members can be found to vote 'yes'.

Article 24 on Functions and Powers is crucial:

1. In order to ensure **prompt and effective action** by the UN, its Members confer on the SC primary [NB not total] responsibility for the maintenance of international peace and security, and agree that in **carrying out its duties** under this responsibility the SC acts on their behalf.
2. In discharging these duties the Security Council shall act **in accordance with the Purposes and Principles of the UN...**
3. The SC shall submit annual and, when necessary, special reports to the GA for its consideration.' [which the GA is bound to 'receive' (C.15) but could refer back critically]

In the light of the SC's toleration of intolerable, vast, wasteful and illegal preparations by the nuclear powers over 47 years, all the emphasised phrases raise issues which could be contested by the GA.

Tolerating and participating in nuclear preparations runs counter to achieving every **Purpose** of the UN, including:

* taking 'effective collective measures for the removal of threats to the peace...and to bring about by peaceful means, and in conformity with the principles of justice and international law,...settlement of international disputes or situations which might lead to a breach of the peace' (C.1.1)
* developing 'friendly relations among nations based on respect for the principle of equal rights and self-determination of peoples, and to take other appropriate measures to strengthen universal peace (C.1.2)
* achieving 'international co-operation in solving international problems..., and in promoting and encouraging respect for human rights and for fundamental freedoms for all (C.1.3).

6) **Principles** include peaceful settlement of disputes (C.2.3), refraining from 'the threat or use of force...in any ...manner inconsistent with the Purposes of the UN (C.2.4), and assisting the UN in taking action in accordance with the Charter (C.2.5).

Thus we can see a way in which, using the legitimacy provided by an initial ICJ reference on nuclear use/threat and given the political will, the global anti-nuclear majority in the General Assembly could mount a very serious challenge to the general domination by the nuclear club. If the nuclear members of the Security Council wanted to challenge the legality of the GA moving into their previous special preserve, it would be open to them to send a reference to the World Court asking for an Advisory Opinion on this point. Alternatively the GA could announce its intended programme of action, recommendations, enforcement schedule, conditional sanctions, and so on and invite the ICJ to advise on its legality.

With its confidence fortified by its alliance with the ICJ on the nuclear question, the GA would have many cards in its hands and could also win the support of other UN agencies. In the event of a period of deadlock the GA's control over the UN budget and over the composition of the other ten members of the SC might well prove critical. The way would be open for the accumulation of such pressures that the nuclear nations would simply have to dismantle their nuclear devices.

Agencies to ensure compliance

As nuclear disarmament becomes increasingly established as a legal obligation, it is logical that it should no longer be left to the nuclear culprits to negotiate - or fail to do so. The UN GA and the Secretary-General would need to create purpose-designed agencies and committees to facilitate and supervise compliance and verification (15), serviced by the Department of Political Affairs, and working in close co-operation with bodies such as the IAEA.

In line with the excellent *McCloy-Zorin Accords* agreed between the US and USSR in 1961 (16), the aim would be to evolve a clear time-framed sequence of rapid concrete steps for mutually balanced and verifiable nuclear disarmament down to zero and beyond (i.e. including dismantling of manufacturing capacities) - and including CBW and other systems as necessary.

These *Compliance Schedules* could be devised for and adapted to various contexts:

1) In an Advisory Opinion the ICJ might recognise a temporary quasi-legality in nuclear possession only on the basis of prompt compliance with each stage in just such a Schedule annexed to its Opinion.

2) If jurisdiction was established in one or more contentious cases which went against the nuclear powers, the ICJ might appoint the official body which had evolved the schedule as Agent of the Court to monitor compliance, facilitate progress and ensure verification, perhaps in conjunction with a new Verification Organisation and an International Atomic Energy Agency with increased powers.

3) Appended to a new treaty.

The relevant UN Commission would be empowered to adjudicate good faith appeals against specific provisions of the Compliance Schedule and help iron out technical difficulties which some nuclear powers might throw up as pretexts for nuclear retention.

In order to reduce fear of cheating and as a confidence-building measure, each main stage of nuclear abolition could be preceded by simultaneous declarations filed independently with the relevant body. In these each nuclear nation would indicate whether or not it was prepared to take the various specific measures pre-stipulated for that stage **if all other nuclear nations also agreed to fulfil their obligations for that stage.** The General Assembly (or SC) would then know against whom to pinpoint any calls for sanctions.

One important precedent is the role of the IAEA. In Iraq after the Gulf war, the IAEA only made its main inspection breakthroughs following tip-offs by Iraqi personnel at the forbidden facilities. A universal anti-nuclear verification regime will certainly involve satellites, scientists and 'national technical means' but it will inspire most confidence if it can found itself on the informed vigilance of millions of ordinary men and women employed at the hundreds of nuclear bases, factories, laboratories, missile silos and uranium processing plants, as well as in countless offices and transport facilities.

The development of proposals for 'citizen verification' as an adjunct to the work of the IAEA is still at a primitive stage. However one could envisage some system of protection for 'whistleblowers' assisting regional verification authorities to identify continuing nuclear violations.

Among the measures which, at each stage, nuclear nations could agree to implement if all the others did, would be to enact pre-specified legislation:

* banning specific activities as contrary to international and domestic law,
* requiring military personnel to arrest those who give them criminal orders, and
* requiring military personnel and employees at specified workplaces to report all activities suspected of contravening the new anti-nuclear legislation.

Part Five: Mobilising for Law and Peace

Former Secretary-General Javier Perez de Cuellar rings the Japanese Peace Bell, in the course of the annual ceremony marking Peace Day. 18 September 1990

UN Photo 176124/Milton Grant

12. Citizens organisations - working our web

To operate the strategy outlined in this Guide, including laying the groundwork for successful references and maximising the educational and diplomatic impact of resulting Advisory Opinions, it is vital that we cooperate:

* with politicians, diplomats and governments of many nations, especially those who are neutral and non-aligned;
* with international civil servants servicing UN agencies and committees, and international groupings such the Non-Aligned Movement and Nuclear-Free Zone Regional Agencies;
* with others actively working on the World Court Poject, creating whatever international, national and specialist groupings of the WCP will help us reach out and network more efficiently.

Along with the image of **net**working we also need the symbol of a **web**. Every group - every society, club, union, guild, municipality, party, institute, small business, cooperative, kinship network, ethnic group, artistic project, band, team, religious community, round table, fraternity, sisterhood.... each can be seen as one node of a **global 'ecological' system**. Together they comprise **world civil society**, a truly vast web of social relations which ought to count much more than it currently does in the overall framework of world organisation, based as it is principally on the nation-state and the multinational company.

In general we can say that just as lawless defence policies threaten to wipe out every human value, so every association defending or reflecting any positive human value has an interest in ensuring a peaceful, unpoisoned world. In a situation where bilateral/multilateral negotiations for radical nuclear disarmament and against proliferation still remain largely ineffective, anti-nuclear advisory rulings can serve what Prof. Richard Falk terms 'educative, focussing and mobilising functions', whereby the civil society of the global community finds its collective voice and dignity over against the pretensions of those who would treat us as global hostages.

By working for **tens of thousands of supporting resolutions and declarations,** we will be giving ourselves a new and different sense of our power and common interest as members of the human family. By paying close attention to the ecology of this vast network we can involve large numbers of groups of all kinds, and encourage them and their fellow members to think creatively about who in turn they are uniquely well-placed to draw in.

SITUATIONS VACANT -

categories of groups who could be engaged in the World Court Project strategy at local, national, regional and global levels.

A PEACE MOVEMENT ORGANISATIONS of all types

B UNITED NATIONS ASSOCIATIONS and World Federalists

C RED CROSS & RED CRESCENT movement

D LEGAL BODIES of all kinds, especially the International Association of Lawyers Against Nuclear Arms (IALANA) and including law firms and academics

E HEALTH/MEDICAL ORGANISATIONS (physical and mental health): especially International Physicians for the Prevention of Nuclear War (IPPNW); medical schools, organisations of nurses, paramedics and preventive health care workers

F SCIENTIFIC ASSOCIATIONS especially the Pugwash Conferences and Science for Peace; unions of scientific workers, research institutes and bodies promoting peaceful use of technology

G Other ACADEMIC, PROFESSIONAL AND VOCATIONAL ASSOCIATIONS, including students' unions and societies

H LABOUR UNIONS AND COOPERATIVES

I POLITICAL PARTIES in government and opposition, especially those such as Greens with explicitly anti-nuclear policies

J LOCAL AUTHORITIES involved in the Nuclear-Free Zone and Peace Messenger Cities movements; also neighbourhood committees, indigenous peoples' councils, provincial level governments and other sub-national entities

K HUMAN RIGHTS groups and leagues, if possible Amnesty International

L ENVIRONMENTAL, green and animal rights bodies

M DEVELOPMENT, AID AND SOLIDARITY ORGANISATIONS

N WOMEN'S ORGANISATIONS, especially Women's International League for Peace and Freedom and Women for Peace; feminist and homosexual rights movements

O ETHNIC ORGANISATIONS and bodies oposing racism and imperialism, associations of migrants and circles of expatriates; INTERNATIONAL FRIENDSHIP, TRAVEL AND EXCHANGE SCHEMES

P Groups representing those specially protected under the laws of war: the ELDERLY, MOTHERS, CHILDREN/YOUTH, PEOPLE WITH A DISABILITY, RELIEF AND EMERGENCY SERVICE WORKERS

Q RELIGIOUS, inter-faith and humanitarian bodies of all types: e.g. World Muslim and Jewish Congresses, World Council of Churches, Catholic Justice and Peace Commissions, World Conference on Religion and Peace

R BUSINESS organisations, institutes and charitable bodies;

S MEDIA organs large and small, printed and audio-visual

T CULTURAL SOCIETIES of all sorts; hobbies, sports and other recreational clubs (could include endorsements by top teams, performers, stars); VOLUNTARY SOCIETIES of all kinds

Involving citizens groups in the World Court Project

By this we mean much more than token support, but rather finding ways to draw in the membership into active, thinking participation, in 5 areas:

Education

* Self-education by core activists concerning international law and the potentials of the UN system, including the ICJ;
* Education of our memberships through articles, promotions and updates in newsletters;
* Public educational work by all the usual methods, including tribunals and teach-ins - perhaps organised jointly with lawyers, medical people, UNAs, sympathetic diplomats;
* New creative forms of witnessing against nuclear crime, such as 'Geneva' poster parades and floats which group together publicly representatives of categories of non-combatants to whom special protection has been accorded under the law of armed conflict. Or publication of cards and posters which put together quotations from the Conventions with corresponding images of specially protected people from around the world. This can be extended to include protected buildings such as clinics, schools and places of worship - where we can request permission to display these 'Geneva' posters.

'Geneva' Poster Parade

In ways such these we can help to awaken people to the universal existence of norms so often taken for granted (noncombatant immunity/right to live without fear of attack) and encourage them to identify across national boundaries as members of a common **civilian estate** having a shared interest in getting the UN system to safeguard our noncombatant rights.

Declarations

* Pass formal resolutions of support for the World Court strategy which declare our group's commitment to do certain specific things, possibly with the provision for an appointed individual or sub-group with a budget to ensure implementation;
* Make a Declaration of the Public Conscience affirming our values and saying how these are menaced by nuclear operations.

Lobbying

* Identify a few decision-makers or influential opinion-formers who are most likely to take our organisation seriously. These might be senior figures in the Ministry of External Affairs, or a member of the ruling party with a power base in our area, or government representatives. It will not be necessary for every group that joins the ICJ-case 'snowball' to contact large numbers of such people; better to concentrate on well-prepared lobbying of just a few, but with persistent follow-up.

In addition a couple of enquiries should suffice to find out which nationals of our country serve on relevant UN bodies other than the General Assembly: notably the Human Rights Committee, WHO Executive, International Law Commission, and environmental bodies.

Outreach

Passive support is better than none, but we should always hope for a **multiplier** effect. Nobody is at the end of the line; everyone already engaged has been reached out to at some point on this issue - and we all know several people who in turn could reach out to others. In fact ordinary people are as indispensable as the experts in mobilising the resources of their unique niche in the ecology of our global civil society. To adapt Hillel: 'If not my group, which group? If not now, when?'

Nor should we be discouraged by lack of media attention in the early stages. We should organise in full appreciation of the potential **exponential growth** of our Project, and aim to transmit this enthusiasm to others who will pass it on. The result will be a kind of 'chain letter' that benefits us all.

In the beginning activists will doubtless start from their own base, in the peace movement or some other progressive group. But our aim will be to work our way:

* **outwards** to more numerous 'unpolitical' and mainstream bodies;
* **upwards** to national and international forums;
* **downwards** to each constituent or affiliated body at the grass roots;
* **across** to similar groups in neighbouring or related districts, regions and countries;

while always being on the alert to encourage 'circuit-jumping' from one kind of network to another.

Even in the nuclear or nuclear-aligned countries, the Project can catch on in very specific ways:

* So far as Use is concerned: who will step forward to argue for its legality? Presumably any such person could have no objection for the matter to be put beyond dispute by the most authoritative 'academy of jurists' in the world.
* So far as Possession and the varying aspects of nuclear Preparations are concerned - in a subsequent phase of the Project - widening support for a World Court reference does not preclude lively national debates on independent versus conditional steps to give effect to the Opinion of the Court.

Communication

Inform others of what the group is doing and planning, what feedback is being received, who we are lobbying and reaching out to; pass around samples of successful resolutions and declarations obtained which other groups can show to those they approach and any specialist literature they have developed for specific constituencies.

Riccarton Neighbourhood Peace Group, New Zealand

Fundraising

As always, this is a vital feature of the campaign. The giant outreach potential of this project offers all manner of income-generating possibilities. They will need to exploited since the cost of the Project is also spiralling.

Of course it is possible that the nuclear powers may succeed in derailing our strategy in some way, or may simply ignore the increased clamour from non-nuclear nations and world opinion. We cannot promise certain success. But we can communicate our genuine excitement that this strategy may well be a way to achieve the anti-nuclear breakthrough which has eluded the world community for over 45 years. Even if there were only a small chance of success, with such an enormous issue at stake surely it should be part of our dignity as citizens of the world not to leave undone any action within our capacity that could make a difference? If we do not speak out our silence will be read as consent. If we do speak out, and lodge our Declarations of the Public Conscience, then the issue will at least not be decided by our own lack of action.

Marching Hibakusha in New York, participating in the SSD I; 1978
Photo: Ittetsu Morishita

13. Declaring the public conscience

It would go too far to suggest that the requirements of the public conscience themselves amount to an additional source of law to stand on an equal footing with the other sources of law mentioned in article 38 of the Statute of the International Court of Justice (see page 49).

But as we saw in the section on the de Martens Clause in Chapter 7, the significance of these dictates is scarcely less great for all that. Through the de Martens clauses included in the *Hague* and *Geneva Conventions*, indications as to the state of public conscience/awareness/values could play a significant role in conditioning the Court's interpretation of the relevance of existing treaties to nuclear 'weapons'. We also saw the importance of 'the demands of the public conscience' in restricting what can be done by way of reprisals (see page 84).

Legal Relevance of Moral Norms

'Natural Law criteria of state behaviour are also applicable through a continued reliance on the de Martens clause, and its invocation of the 'laws of humanity' and 'the dictates of the public conscience'. Such a moral outreach **within international law** makes it important and entirely appropriate to consider for **legal relevance** the great variety of statements by religious bodies describing their urgent concern and supporting reasoning about the irreconcilability of current doctrines pertaining to the use of nuclear weapons and the dictates of public conscience...Such materials by religious bodies or international jurists are not law as such, but **evidence** as to the content of law, especially given the legal **duty** by governments to respect the dictates of the public conscience in their war-making activities.

- Judgment of London Nuclear Warfare Tribunal, section 1.2.4

(emphasis in original)

Normally the Court is only empowered to deal with States and other inter-governmental organisations. However there are various ways in which our Declarations of the Public Conscience could be placed before it, for it to give them whatever legal significance it may decide on:

Route (a) Article 65.2 of the Statute of the ICJ lays down that advisory opinions must be requested in writing with an exact statement of the question 'accompanied by **all documents likely to throw light upon the question.**'

Route (b) Individual states may submit written statements, to which any number of 'Declarations of the Public Conscience' could be appended.

Route (c) International organisations such as ECOSOC or the Human Rights Committee who are considered by the Court as 'likely to be able to furnish information on the question' will also be asked for their views. In turn they would notify any NGOs who are in official consultative status with them and who might have submissions to make. For example, it would be entirely appropriate for IPPNW to ask WHO to forward to the ICJ tens of thousands of 'de Martens declarations' from health workers around the world, to whom special protection has been accorded in the Geneva Conventions, and who thus have a special moral authority to call on the Court for protection. A special moral authority would also attach to declarations lodged by organisations representing other 'Genevans', such as sick and infirm, especially disabled war veterans, pregnant women and nursing mothers, children, the elderly, relief and emergency service workers.

Route (d) In the US and some other countries courts have 'inherent jurisdiction' to receive and consider communications from expert and other third parties known as 'Brandeis briefs' (after Judge Brandeis). These are also called 'amicus briefs', since they are presented as coming from 'friends of the Court' to help it to understand more deeply and thus fulfil its function of doing justice. Since we are all individually subject to international law, there would theoretically be nothing to stop the Court from considering itself able to receive individual and collective 'amicus briefs' from well-wishing citizens loyal to the ideals of the UN, organisations of expert professionals, United Nations Associations, and so forth.

As a rule, however, (a) to (c) above will be better routes to the Court, lest the nuclear powers try to pretend that the Court is being unduly influenced by 'biased political lobbying'.

'The law is not static, but undergoes continual adaptation to the needs of a changing world.' (*Nuremberg Judgment*). An era of continuing global peril (nowadays especially in terms of dangers from proliferation) demands an exceptional response in the shape of an exceptional number of declarations gathered from every kind of citizens group and from every region of the world. As we invite ever-wider circles of people to contribute to this project - which to many must seem impossibly ambitious in terms of size and time-scale - we can draw on the 'de Martens' idea to explain why everyone and every group really can make a difference, how their personal beliefs really can weigh on the Scales of Justice. Provided they declare them!

At the same time we should reassure people that no special expertise in the law is needed for them to lodge legally-significant declarations of their values and awareness in respect of the nuclear menace. 'Like a petition, only with a clearer legal relevance', we can explain, adding that the Declarations will be carefully stored and eventually - when the World Court has been asked to give its advisory ruling- arrangements will be made for them all to be delivered (in one of the ways specified above) to the Palace of Peace at the Hague where the Court sits. Truckloads!

We can also explain that in the meantime they will be catalogued under type and location of organisation, etc which will help us to assess, plan and promote the growth of the Project. Groups and even individuals can choose whether to endorse or adapt a standard model declaration or whether to write their own from scratch. If they choose to write their own, we should encourage them to **write from the heart**, but remind them to avoid language which could be dismissed as 'political' e.g. if it just blames a single nuclear nation.

Organisations preparing a campaign to collect Declarations of the Public Conscience, may like to bear in mind the following points:

a) As affirmations before the world, the declarations have an intrinsic authority which can only be diluted if we address them explicitly to the ICJ (or to the UN or a specific government).

b) The declarations - or copies, or the fact of their existence - could also be given a valuable subsidiary use: building support for the ICJ-reference proposal, among NGOs, among governments and in various parts of the UN machinery.

c) However we should beware of the political tail wagging the legal dog. In particular it may be a mistake to seek to tailor the wording of our Declarations to any particular phase of a complex legal-political process, e.g. getting governments to vote for Phase 1 of this process, a reference on Use/Threat. If the mere existence of devices of mass destruction affronts our values, we should say so. It will not detract from the immediate lobbying utility of our Declarations in the initial phase. On the other hand if we only focus on Use, this will certainly undermine the value of our declarations as evidence of an emergent global consensus against Possession, which is the later part of the journey towards total Elimination, and the part where declarations by governments and NGOs will be most needed.

d) Experience in the UK, and previously in cases in the Netherlands and the US, suggests that in return for well-produced documentation many people may be prepared to contribute financially to support the campaign. Therefore any declarations or 'amicus briefs' which we design ready for signature should be accompanied by (and repeated in) a longer explanatory brochure with

   * information on supporters to date;
   * an opportunity for people to ask for follow-up information, updates and other assistance in spreading the word;
   * an opportunity for people to contribute financially.

Sample declaration used in pilot-project in Brighton, UK, Winter 1991

WORLD COURT PROJECT
DECLARATION OF PUBLIC CONSCIENCE

By

of

1. I affirm before the world my right to live in peace in a safe unpoisoned environment and my responsibility to secure my rights by upholding common morality and legal order.
2. I consider that all nuclear weapons threaten my peace of mind and the security of my loved ones. For all the people of the earth they spell only fear and suffering, grief and death.
3. Wherever and however these weapons are exploded, their poisonous fallout could affect every person, every nation, and every species and bring cumulative damage to generations unborn.
4. If I have a quarrel with my neighbours, I do not attack those who are not attacking anyone; nor do I threaten to destroy the neighbourhood.
5. I therefore hold that unleashing indiscriminate devastation would betray the very values nuclear preparations are supposed to safeguard.
6. I declare that nothing could ever justify inflicting such destruction. Any state willing to use nuclear weapons would be acting in a way that was irresponsible, immoral, and criminal.
7. **I therefore call upon all governments to bring one or more motions to the United Nations asking the International Court of Justice to pronounce on the legality or otherwise of nuclear weapons.**
8. I make this solemn declaration with no hidden political motives, and no hostility towards the inhabitants of any nation.

Signed –　　　　　　　　　　Date –

14. Role of lawyers

Most societies are organised on the basis of an extremely specialised division of labour. Few of us know much about the working situation of those in other walks of life. 'Peace people' here, lawyers there and diplomats in another box again - this has been the usual pattern.

But in this Project we need to reach out to meet each other and learn from each other. Although initial contacts may be made hurriedly in the interval of a political meeting or at a diplomatic reception, part of the challenge will be to create venues and occasions for more profound dialogue, leading to trust-building and business-like co-operation. This will take time.

Many lawyers and diplomats may be put off by what they see as excessive informality, or wonder whether peace workers will prove unreliable or indiscreet. Likewise activists may find that it takes a while before they find diplomats who aren't suspicious of us, or lawyers who make room in their crowded diaries for serious ICJ case work. Professional lawyers, like the rest of us, have their own priorities and preoccupations. Some will eagerly value initiatives of the kind represented by this project. Others will need to be encouraged, persuaded or challenged. Many of the most committed lawyers are overwhelmed with responding to the latest attacks on labour organisers, women's centres or peasant co-operatives. They will sign petitions when asked, but with the best will in the world, simply can't take on any further burdens. They may lead us to others better placed to join or start a group of lawyers for a World Court reference.

What lawyers can do

We can look to lawyers to:

a) produce detailed legal briefings on subjects such as nuclearism, the advisory jurisdiction of the ICJ and the legal value of declarations;

b) prepare compilations of 'the laws of humanity' stigmatising plans and threats to poison or otherwise murder harmless people - which should include a dosier of all those parts of their national legal codes which could be brought against such activities if carried out by ordinary citizens;

c) identify, approach and seek to involve 'the most highly qualified publicists' - make compilations of their teachings;

d) use their knowledge and professional authority to educate public opinion and progressive organisations, e.g. through tribunals and teach-ins in connection with the UN Decade of International Law - possibly organised jointly with local sections of IPPNW or UNA, student unions, etc;

e) identify key national and international legal organisations and make concrete plans for educating them and getting them involved - at first progressive lawyers may prefer to reach out to diplomats or the general public, but their biggest contribution will be to tackle their own profession;

f) identify key politicians, members of the government, legal advisers to Foreign Ministries and the embassies of key nations; either one to one, or as a group of lawyers, or in mixed lawyer/lay delegations, approach them for discussion of the ICJ-reference strategy; encourage them to conduct detailed reviews of past diplomatic practice in order to identify any omissions which could be taken to imply legal acceptance of the 'Balance of Terror'; draft declarations and resolutions repudiating the legality and alleged 'customary' status of nuclearism;

g) network within IALANA and other organisations to ensure high priority for the ICJ-case and business-like work at and between events.

h) identify and lobby those who can nominate candidates for election to the ICJ and help to keep Foreign Offices informed of the records of the various candidates; identify fellow nationals serving on the International Law Commission, Human Rights Committee, Sixth Committee, etc and approach them as fellow professionals.

HAGUE DECLARATION OF 1st WORLD CONGRESS OF IALANA, Sept 24, 1989

(extracts)

The International Association of Lawyers Against Nuclear Arms.affirming that the use or threat of use of nuclear weapons is a war crime and a crime against humanity, as well as a gross violation of other norms of international customary and treaty law and envisioning as an urgent task the total outlawing of nuclear weapons, including their research, manufacture and possession * *(see below)*;...

invites lawyers throughout the world to sensitize 'the public conscience' to the incompatibility of nuclear weapons with international law and to utilize their respective legal processes to build up a body of law dealing with various aspects of the problem;

calls upon all Governments to conduct their international relations and their military planning in accordance with the mandates of the United Nations Charter, especially article 2 (4), and the laws of war and other relevant principles and rules of international law, including those relating to the rights of neutral states, the rights to life, peace and development, genocide, the environment, self-determination, non-intervention, and other human and people's rights; (...)

appeals to the Governments of all States Members of the UN to take immediate steps towards obtaining a resolution by the UN Assembly under article 96 of the UN Charter, requesting the International Court of Justice to render an advisory opinion on the illegality of the use of nuclear weapons;

dedicates itself to the enunciation and promotion of the rights of life and to peace as the most fundamental of all human rights...

(Note that at its Berlin Colloquium in Nov, 1990, IALANA made clear that this explicit outlawing should take place by means of treaties and resolutions confirmatory of* ***existing*** *customary international law.)*

United Nations, Geneva

Conference of the Eighteen Nation Committee on Disarmament. Here delegates are seen standing in the lobby prior to entering the Council Chamber for the meeting.

Photo: UN/hfj

15. Working with politicians and diplomats

Politicians are usually responsive to pressure from below. To what extent depends on how well-organised is the pressure and whether it appears to represent a constituency powerful enough to sway significant votes at election time. One of the greatest difficulties for the contemporary peace movement is that in the West at least, military and specifically nuclear defence issues no longer generate much political attention - except in so far as they can be used to whip up nationalist sentiment at critical moments or to attack promoters of the Peace Dividend with the scare of job losses in defence industries. It is therefore vital that any approaches made to politicians or political parties on the legal plane - at any level all the way from municipalities and provinces to international forums such as the EC or federations such as the Socialist International - be coupled with practical proposals for implementation which can be used when 'selling' the policy to the voters. This approach is also likely to win allies within peace and other progressive movements and party caucuses who may be sceptical of a purely 'legalistic' approach.

Diplomats by contrast are essentially government civil servants and carry their political masters' instructions in their back pockets. They are usually powerless in foreign policy formulation - at least overtly. Nevertheless they can be useful channels through which to pass messages to distant governments and are often better informed than government officials on the detail of inter-governmental negotiations. They can be at least as responsive to dialogue with NGOs. Naturally on matters as delicate as nuclear defence strategy diplomats will be reluctant to take firm positions until clear directives have been received from the relevant ministries back home.

Thus the primary work of convincing governments to support the World Court initiative has to be at the national level, through patient work in party policy groups and direct approaches to key politicians (not only in Defence but also Foreign Affairs, Legal and even Health Departments). Nevertheless the opportunities for exploring the nuances of particular positions with diplomats both at home and abroad should not be neglected. In particular, embassies and UN missions alike represent important locations for discussion with foreign governments and for the elaboration of tactical alliances between states - a necessary development if the Project is to succeed.

A number of guidelines are offered to those considering international approaches in the diplomatic world on behalf of the Project:

* Lobbyists should be sensitive to norms of protocol, dress and professionalism observed by the diplomatic community worldwide.
* In particular, an understanding should be reached early in the discussion regarding confidentiality, since publicity of individual viewpoints, or of tentative shifts within particular ministries for example, could be damaging to the progress of the dialogue.
* Ideally at least one lawyer and one national of the country concerned should be present in the delegation; this is especially the case where lobbyists might be perceived as 'representing' nuclear and/or colonial powers.
* It makes sense to arrange follow-up visits or other contact to keep the issue alive and find out what instructions have been received from government ministers.
* Subject to the caveat above regarding confidentiality, contact should be made with sympathetic groups in the relevant country with a view to encouraging the lobbying process at the national level and concerting efforts with those working internationally.
* Colleagues in the network should be kept informed of contacts made and responses received. This will avoid duplication of effort and will sharpen subsequent approaches to the same government, since their specific concerns can be anticipated.

No matter how the problem is raised with representatives of non-nuclear states, sooner or later objections will be put forward which are in the realm of realpolitik rather than law. Even among countries well-known for their anti-nuclear positions, such as Mexico and certain partners in the Non-Aligned Movement, the fear exists that pressure, covert or overt, financial or political, will eventually be exerted by the nuclear weapons states - notably but not solely the USA - to abandon this challenge to nuclearism. Furthermore in the case of states such as India, Pakistan, the Koreas and many Arab countries, there is frequently a lack of trust in regional peace processes, leading to reluctance to abandon nuclear options, whether yet fully exercised or not.

The answer to both problems must be an approach based on **collective security strategies**. In the case of nuclear weapons state opposition, the objective should be to secure a resolution requesting an ICJ opinion **co-sponsored** by several states jointly (cf. the Six-Nations Initiative of the early 1980s), **supported** by several dozen more, and **voted** by a resounding majority in the relevant requesting body. In this way no single state can be picked off for retribution and the Court would have difficulty dodging the question. This is the virtue of an approach echoing the 'Indian resolution' voted overwhelmingly by the GA every year for the past decade.

In the case of nuclear rivalry in the regional context **joint sponsorship** of the resolution could conceivably be one of relatively few positions agreeable by all sides. This in itself would act as an important confidence-building measure, provided the non-discriminatory character of the initiative is forcefully spelled out, and provided the move goes hand in hand with other measures at the political level seriously to tackle the underlying tensions, and also to ban all other weapons of mass destruction.

The primary demand to be made of politicians, government officials and diplomats alike is the issuing of **anti-nuclear declarations**. These will help build a climate of international opinion favourable to the framing of a request to the ICJ for an Opinion on what is after all a highly sensitive question. Such declarations are essential if the Court is to feel that it is articulating the generally-held views of both public and governments. Otherwise it will be tempted to refer the question to the Security Council, a step that would either advance us no further or worse, seriously set us back.

Declarations by governments can be in the form of diplomatic notes, communiqués, resolutions or statements made in international forums. They will need to be grounded in the contemporary context of worldwide concern over proliferation of nuclear devices and trained personnel, and should reflect the growing consensus - at least among enlightened expert opinion - that nuclear strategies and systems are antiquated, dangerous and impractical, as well as criminal, methods of defence. Furthermore, declarations may need to stress that any previous failure to confront the illegality of nuclearism should not be read as acquiescence, nor implying that the practices of a small minority of states should be regarded as in any way settled, recognised or customary.

If a sufficient number of such statements of principle can be elicited, the beginnings of a new understanding of 'State Practice' will be established, and the foundations of an inter-state anti-nuclear coalition laid down. The great advantage of the ICJ reference is that it provides the occasion for a **non-discriminatory** question to be raised with many governments simultaneously.

The obstacles encountered when dealing with representatives of nuclear weapons states are of a different order and type. Given the huge political, human and financial investments made by them in these genocidal systems, and given the absence at this time in history of powerful oppositional movements able to dictate disarmament measures, the most promising line of approach must undoubtedly lie in stressing the dangers of further proliferation should their present course be continued. The case of Iraqi nuclear programme has graphically illustrated the risks involved in exporting, not only the technology of mass destruction, but also the doctrine of deterrence, by which any nation can claim the God-given right to threaten the globe with radioactive incineration in the name of national security. Given the spread of both nuclear devices and know-how, and the weakness of the Non-Proliferation regime, it cannot be many decades before all the world's major regional powers - not to mention sub-national or 'terrorist' organisations - are fully engaged in the race for nuclear dominance. As Erich Geiringer argues in his recent IPPNW briefing paper *'Death of a Salesman'*, the World Court Project offers the current nuclear weapons states a graceful exit from their appalling dilemma:

> 'The notion that a judicious mixture of threats and promises, cash and new technologies, covert action and secret deals, combined with assiduous door-to-door selling of the American way of life, will persuade the world to leave nukes in Uncle Sam's capable hands, is a dangerous misreading of post Cold War reality ...
>
> 'Proliferative pressure is great. Even if she had the wherewithal to engage in a series of preventive war à la Gulf, America would not be able to carry the world community or her own people along in such ventures. A less drastic preventive regime is urgently needed ...
>
> 'The USA no longer has enough carrots or big enough stick to placate a world seething with ethnic conflicts ... Peace will depend on equitable rules, administered and enforced by the world community ...
>
> 'From now on only law, inspection and enforcement can keep proliferation in check and these cannot be put in place on a discriminatory basis. World security depends on the setting up of a UN control agency with powers involving a partial surrender of national sovereignty in favour of collective security ...
>
> 'America could accept that any **use** of nuclear weapons would now be against the law of nations; that she and other nuclear powers have the right to maintain, **but not to enlarge**, their nuclear stockpiles until

they can be phased out by negotiation, convention and treaty; and that meanwhile a **nuclear freeze** will be enforced by the UN with the support of America and the other nuclear powers ...

'She must obey the law she wishes to impose on the non-nuclear nations. They will no longer play the NPT game without a guarantee that the nuclear powers are stopping vertical proliferation, including the deployment of anti-nuclear defences which would enable states to plot nuclear blackmail behind an anti-nuclear shield ...

'The US must either join the anti-nuclear camp or take on single-handedly the Hydra of Proliferation and a world unwilling to concede her nuclear hegemony; must agree that the use of nuclear weapons is forbidden or cast herself in the lonely and doomed role of a nuclear overlord.

'Time is short. Any reasonable computation based on election cycles, economic forecasts and technological data would conclude that little more than a decade will decide whether the genie can be returned to its bottle or whether we shall enter a dark age of nuclear terror.'

'Over the longer-term, therefore, it is desirable that the possession of nuclear weapons be judged illegal, under an advisory opinion of the ICJ. It is sometimes contended that this would fail to advance nuclear disarmament but rather succeed in debasing international law through being demonstrably ineffective. But the odium which a widely accepted declaration of illegality would entail, would be likely to quarantine the nuclear cancer, making it clear that nuclear weapons were extraneous to the Charter and collective security, and strengthening the political impulse towards nuclear disarmament.'

Dr Kennedy Graham,
Secretary-General of Parliamentarians Global Action, June 1991.

Evening glow over Hiroshima. 1945. Woodcut print: Kiyoshi Asai, then aged 44, since deceased.

Part Six: Reference Section

Notes to text

Part 1

1. Delf; Dewar; Foundation *'Ban Cruise Missiles'*.
2. Delf, ch.13.
3. Of course slavery, child labour and so forth persist in many parts of the world.
4. Dunn; Midgley.
5. Dunn.
6. Jayatilleke; Sastri; Weil.
7. Weeramantry, pp.71, 79; Mahmassani, p.302.
8. Midgley.
9. Dower.
10. KABSRAJ.
11. Best, p.149ff.
12. Pal.
13. McKee.
14. Bacque.
15. Falk, 1986, ch.1.
16. Van den Biesen and Ingelse; Foundation *'Ban Cruise Missiles'*.
17. Singh and McWhinney.
18. Boyle, 1986b.
19. Bertell, p.330.
20. Pax Legalis: Zelter and Bhardwaj
21. Delf, p.9.
22. London Nuclear Warfare Tribunal.
23. Dupuy.
24. USSR Praesidium Decree.
25. Hickman, J. Ch.12 of Dewar.
26. Clark.
27. Barnaby.

Part 2

1. Campbell, T. ch.5 of Dewar.
2. McWhinney, 1984; Falk, 1986.
3. Akehurst, p.8; Sims.
4. London Nuclear Warfare Tribunal.
5. Weeramantry, p.65.
6. Covert Action Information Bulletin, 1987a.
7. Lange.
8. McNair.
9. Brownlie, 1990, p.513; 1979, p.20.
10. Brownlie, 1983, p.370.
11. *Trial of German Major War Criminals*, p.497.
12. Brownlie, 1983, p.35ff.
13. Reprinted in Brownlie, 1983, p.387.
14. Rosenne.
15. See articles by Singh, de Lacharrière and Lachs in Sturgess and Chubb, pp.453,457,468.
16. McDougal and Feliciano.
17. p.71, reaffirmed in *Western Sahara*, 1975, p.19.
18. This section draws heavily on McWhinney, 1990, and to some extent on Falk, 1986.
19. McWhinney.
20. Falk, 1986, p.15.
21. *Certain Expenses of the UN*.
22. McWhinney, 1990, p.176ff.
23. Falk, 1986, pp.171-2.
24. *Namibia*, 1971, p.27; *Western Sahara*, p.19.
25. ICJ Reports, 1984, pp.169,392; 1986, p.14.
26. *Western Sahara*, pp.19-21.
27. See also opinion of Judge Lacks, ICP Rep, 1976, pp.19ff.
28. ICJ Rep, 1984, p.436.
29. And even the General Assembly might get round this, see ch 11.
30. Singh and McWhinney, p.94ff.
31. Brownlie, 1963, p.273.

32. *Nicaragua*, ICJ Rep, 1986, paras. 195,211.
33. *The Caroline*
34. *Trial of German Major War Criminals*, p.436.
35. Singh and McWhinney, p.58ff.
36. ibid. pp.69-79.
37. Spaight, pp.271ff.
38. McKee.
39. Alperovitz, p.285; Sherwin.
40. Spaight, pp.274,276.
41. Builder and Graubard.
42. London Nuclear Warfare Tribunal, para. 3.3.2.
43. Brownlie, 1965, p.450.
44. Van den Biesen and Ingelse, p.86.
45. *Milch Trial*, p.64.
46. *Hostages Traial*, p.34.
47. Brierly, p.319.

Part 3

1. Foundation 'Ban Cruise Missiles'.
2. Brownlie, 1963, p.263; Findlay,M in Evans.
3. Goldblat, p.193.
4. *Krupp Trial*, p.133.
5. *Nicaragua*, 1971.
6. Brownlie, 1965, p.449; Grief (a), p.38.
7. 16 UN GAOR Supp No 17, UN Doc A/4942 Add 3, reprinted in Singh and McWhinney, p.407 and Schindler and Toman.
8. Reprinted in Schindler and Toman.
9. UN GAOR Supp No 47, Doc A/38/648.
10. Resolution passed by GA Oct 1991.
11. Goldblat, pp.150, 159, 162, 175.
12. Grief (a), p.24.
13. Falk, 1965.
14. Singh and McWhinney, p.304.
15. ibid. p.123.

16. Goldblat, pp.145-6.
17. Spaight, p.276; Stone, p.343; Schwarzenberger, 1958, pp.26-28; 1968, Vol.1, pp.194-199; Singh and McWhinney, pp.121-129, 310-311; Brownlie, 1965, p.442; Castren, 1971, p.98.
18. Roberts and Guelff, p.462.
19. Walzer.
20. eg, Casablanca Directive of Combined Chiefs of Staff, Jan 1943.
21. eg. Edinburgh Resolution 1969, reprinted in Singh and McWhinney, p.411.
22. Schindler and Toman, p.203.
23. Bertell; Chazov.
24. Weeramantry, p.95.
25. Pictet, esp. Vol.4.
26. Even Singh and McWhinney (pp.1540-55) are misleading here and actually reprint paras 1 and 4 in direct quotation with no indication that paras 2 and 3 have been omitted.
27. UN Treaty Series Vol.75, 1950, Treaty 973.
28. Cited in Hearn, p.242; see also Grief (a), p.25ff.
29. Brownlie, 1983, p.250.
30. ibid. p.257.
31. IALANA Congress: papers by Mullerson and van Boven.
32. Singh and McWhinney, pp.207-209.
33. Nanda and Lowe, p.92.
34. Castren, 1954.
35. 16 UN GAOR pp.505-7, UN Doc A/PV 1043.
36. 3 UNRIAA p.1938.
37. 12 UNRIAA p.281.
38. Goldblat, p.157.
39. Reprinted in ICJ Pleadings 1973 and 11 ILM 1972, p.1416.
40. 14 UNGAOR A/8730, p.278, UN Doc A/Conf 4816.
41. Brownlie, 1983, p.248.
42. ibid. p.127.
43. Weeramantry, p.129.
44. Roberts and Guelff, p.340.

45. IALANA Congress papers by van Boven and Bhagwati.
46. Roberts and Guelff, p.144.
47. Arangio-Ruiz, p.36.
48. McDermott, in Evans.
49. De Vattel, section 347.
50. Arangio-Ruiz, p.16.
51. ibid. pp.25 and 43-44.
52. *Barcelona Traction*, p.3.
53. St John.
54. Falk et al, 1982.
55. Sen Jackson, 'Time', Jan 28 1980.
56. Daniel Ellsberg, former top Pentagon nuclear strategist, in Conservation Press, Berkeley, 1980.
57. Brownlie, 1963, pp.364, 431.
58. Atlantic Declaration 1942, Preamble to 1948 UN Declaration of Human Rights.
59. Even Sadurska, who believes threats can help to deter violence, has to admit that 'this is a precarious game' and that 'an environment in which threats of force are regularly used is likely to be very unstable.' (pp.247 and 250).
60. Res 46/37D, among others.
61. p.19, US Lawyers Committee first emphasis added.
62. Hearn, p.213.
63. Bacque.
64. Galtung.
65. Chomsky, p65 El Salvador and Nicaragua Solidarity Campaigns.
66. Hearn, p.222; Shaw,M in Pogany, p.2.
67. Grief (a), pp.41-42; Arbess,D *'The International Law of Armed Conflict in the light of Contemporary Deterrence Strategies'*, McGill Law Jnl, Vol 30, 1985, p.89 and pp.107-121.
68. US Lawyers Committee on Nuclear Policy, p.21.
69. Fr. Richard McSorley, SJ, quoted in MacBride in Introduction to van den Biesen and Ingelse.

70. Boyle, 1986, p.1444.
71. Weeramantry, p.136.
72. Grinyer and Smoker.
73. Mothersson.
74. Covert Action Information Bulletin, 1987b.
75. For a list of serious accidents involving US nuclear weapons, see Goldblat, pp.77-79.
76. Schell, 1982.
77. Grinyer and Smoker.
78. Schell, 1984.
79. Lackey,D. 'Immoral Risks' in Social Philosophy and Policy.
80. Cited in Oppenheim, International Law 6th ed., 1940, Vol.II, p.276.
81. *Corfu Channel*, pp.34-35; Singh and McWhinney, p.191.
82. Schindler and Toman, p.823.
83. Bertell.
84. Schell, 1983; Falk and Lifton.
85. General Comment 6(16) article 6: Report of the Human Rights Committee, 37 UN GAOR Supp No 40, 1982.
86. General Comment 14(23) article 6: Report of the Human Rights Committee, 40 UN GAOR Supp No 40, 1985.
87. GA Resolution 2542 (XXIV), GAOR (1829 meeting), 1969.
88. Bertell; Falk and Lifton.
89. *Tunis-Morocco Nationality Decrees.*
90. Boyle, 1986, pp.1419-1424.
91. ibid. p.1445.
92. Especially since some of them claim that their nuclear 'defence' posture will remain non-negotiable (apart from its details), irrespective of the actions of other countries.
93. Boyle, 1986, p.1445.
94. Boyle, 1986b.
95. Goldblat, p.172.
96. St John.
97. Boyle, 1986, p.1446.

98. The Nazi-Soviet Pact to carve up Poland would be an example of another treaty that was void for breach of a norm of *jus cogens*.
99. Goldblat, p.157.
100. Grief (b).
101. De Jure Belli ac Pacis, 1625.
102. Bertell, p.44, citing also her 'Ionising Radiation Exposure and Human Species Survival', Canadian Environmental Health Review, Vol.25, 2, June 1981.
103. Among eminent authorities cited by Bertell are: Hermann Muller, 'Radiation and Heredity', American Journal of Public Health, Vol.54, 1, 1964, pp.42-50; Karl Z Morgan, 'Hazards of Low-Level Radiation', Yearbook of Science and the Future, Supplement to Encyclopaedia, 1980.

Part 4

1. Acheson, p.13; Rostow, p.264; US State Dept statement.
2. Falk, 1986; McWhinney, 1990.
3. Even Before the Bomb Drops, 1988 information pack written by Dr Robin Stott for the Medical Campaign Against Nuclear Weapons (now MEDACT), 601 Holloway Road, London N19 4DJ, UK.
4. Effects of Nuclear War on Health and Health Services, WHO, Geneva, 1987.
5. McWhinney, 1990, p.44 - referring to the inspired dissenting opinion of US Judge Jessup in 1966, who argues that the Court should take judicial notice of the accumulation of expressions of condemnation of Apartheid. (ICJ Reports, 1976, p.323.)
6. Lord Talbot in *Barbuit's Case*, 1735 25 ER 777.
7. British Manual of Military Law, Part 1, ch.VI, para 23 and part 3, p.177, HMSO; Boyle 1986, pp.1429-30.
8. Mothersson.
9. UNTS Vol.605, p.205.
10. Barnaby (ed).
11. Lange; Blum.
12. Singh and McWhinney, p.214ff.
13. GA Res. 1991 (XVIII).

14. Although the Charter assigns many *peace-keeping* functions primarily to the Security Council, many *law-enforcement* functions can be led by the Secretary-General on behalf of the GA. (Falk, 1986.)
15. See the work of the Markland Group, Hamilton, Canada.
16. Goldblat, p.153; London Nuclear Warfare Tribunal, Appendix B.

Bibliography

(Items marked * are especially recommended)

Alperovitz, Gar: *Atomic Diplomacy*, revised ed, London 1985

Acheson, D: [remarks on Cuba missiles crisis], *Proceedings of the American Society of Intl. Law*, 1963

Akehurst, M: *A Modern Introduction to Intl. Law*; 4th ed 1982

Allot, Philip: *Intl. Law and Intl. Revolution: Reconceiving the World*; Josephine Onoh Memorial Lecture, Hull Univ Press, UK, 1989

Arangio-Ruiz, Gaetano (Rapporteur): *Third Report [to the General Assembly] on State Responsbility for the International Law Commission of the UN*, 1991; A/CN.4/440

Arbess, Daniel J: *The Intl. Law of Armed Conflict in the Light of Contemporary Deterrence Strategies*; McGill Law Jnl, vol 30, 1985, p89 at pp107-121)

Barnaby, Frank (ed): *Building a More Democratic United Nations* (CAMDUN-1 conference proceedings); Frank Cass, London 1991

Bacque, James: *Other Losses*, 1989

Bertell, Rosalie: *No Immediate Danger - Prognosis for a Radioactive Earth*; The Women's Press, London 1985

Best, Geoffrey: *Humanity in Warfare*; London 1983

Blum, William: *The CIA, a Forgotten History*; Zed Press, London and New Jersey, 1988

Brierly, JL: *The Law of Nations*, 5th ed, 1955

Brownlie, Ian: *The Use of Force by States*; Oxford 1963

: *Some Legal Aspects of the Use of Nuclear Weapons*; Intl. Law Comparative Qtly, vol 14, p 437, 1965

: *Principles of Public Intl. Law*, 3rd ed; Oxford 1979; 4th ed 1990

: *(ed.) *Basic Documents in Intl. Law*; Oxford 1983 (contains UN Charter, ICJ Statute, Human Rights treaties, Law of Sea, Vienna Convention on Treaties,etc)

Boyle, Francis: *World Politics and Intl. Law*; Duke University, US, 1985

: * *The Relevance of Intl. Law to the 'Paradox' of Nuclear Deterrence*; Northwestern University Law Review, Vol 80,6, 1986

: *Defending Civil Resistance under Intl. Law*; Salem, Oregon 1986 b

Builder, C and Graubard, M: *The Intl. Law of Armed Conflict: Implications for the Concept of Assured Destruction*; Rand Corporation paper, 1983

Castren, Erik: *The Present Law of War and Neutrality*; Helsinki, 1954

: *Illegality of Nuclear Weapons*, Toledo Law Review, 1971

Caulfield, C: *Multiple Exposures - Chronicles of the Radiation Age*; London 1989

Chazov, Yevgeni et al: *Nuclear War: The Medical and Biological Consequences*, Moscow, 1984

Chomsky, Noam: *Strategic Arms, the Cold War and the Third World, in 'Exterminism and the Cold War'*, London 1982

Clark, Ramsay: *War Crimes - A Report on US War Crimes in Iraq*; New York 1992. From: 36 E. 12th St, 6th fl, NY 10003

Covert Action Information Bulletin

: *CIA and Drugs, Vol 28*; Washington DC, 1987 a

: *Special Issue on the Religious Right*, 1987 b

Delf, George: * *Humanizing Hell - The Law vs. Nuclear Weapons*; Hamish Hamilton, London 1985

Dewar, John et al (eds): *Nuclear Weapons, The Peace Movement and the Law*, MacMillan, Basingstoke, UK 1986

Dower, John: *War Without Mercy - Race and Power in the Pacific War*; London 1986

Dunn, Ted (ed): *The Ecology of a Peaceful World*; Swansea, UK 1975

Dupuy, RG: *The Future of the Intl. Law of the Environment*: Hague Academy Workshop, 1984; Dordrecht, 1985

Elias, T O: *How the ICJ Deals With Requests for Advisory Opinions, in Makarczyk (ed): Essays in Intl. Law in Honour of Judge Manfred Lachs*; 1984

Evans, Harold: *Open Letter to Prime Ministers of Australia, New Zealand*, 1987; 53a Hackthorne Rd, Christchurch, NZ

Falk, Richard: *The Shimoda Case: a legal appraisal of the Atomic Attacks upon: Hiroshima and Nagasaki*; 59 Am J of Intl. Law, p 751, 1965

: *The End of World Order*; New York 1983

: * *Reviving the World Court*; Vancouver 1986

: (et al) *Studies on a Just World Order*; Boulder, Colorado, 1982

Falk R, Meyrowitz L and Sanderson J: *Nuclear Weapons and Intl. Law*, Princeton Centre of Intl. Studies Occasional paper No. 10, 1981

Falk R and Lifton, Robert J: *Indefensible Weapons*; NY 1983

Foundation 'Ban the Cruise Missiles': *Cruise Missile Proceedings in the Netherlands, A Model for Collective Litigation*, Amsterdam, 1990

Galtung, Johann: *There Are Alternatives! Four Roads to Peace and Security*; Nottingham, UK 1984

Goldblat, Jozef: *Agreements for Arms Control*; London, 1982

Grief, Nicholas: * (a)*The Illegality of Nuclear Weapons*; p 22 of Pogany, I (ed), below

: (b) *Nuclear Tests and Intl. Law*; p 217 of Pogany, I (ed) below

: *Memorandum on World Court Project*, IALANA, 1992.

Grinyer, Ann and Smoker, Paul: *It Couldn't Happen, Could It? A Study of the Dangers of Accidental Nuclear War*; Richardson Institute, Lancaster Univ, 1987

Hearn, William R: *The Intl. Legal Regime Regulating Nuclear Deterrence and Warfare*; British Yearbook of Intl. Law, Vol 61, p 199, 1990

HMSO: [British] *Manual of Military Law; London*, 1958

IALANA: * *1989 Congress papers*: Denver Jnl of Intl. Law and Policy, Vol 19,1, 1990

Jaipal, Rikhi: * *Nuclear Arms and the Human Race*; Allied, New Delhi, 1986

Jayatilleke, KN: *Principles of Intl. Law in Buddhist Doctrine*; 120 Hague Receuil p 445, 1967

Just Defence: *Charter*, newsletter and occasional papers; The Vicarage, Appleby, Cumbria, CA16 6QW, UK

Kenny, A: *The Logic of Deterrence*, London 1985

KABSRAJ Korean Atomic Bomb Sufferers Relief Association of Japan: *The 20,000 Forgotten Survivors*; Osaka, 1975. (16pp, photocopy from IPB)

Keith, Sir K: *The extent of the Advisory Jurisdiction of the Intl. Court of Justice*; AW Sithoff, Leyden, 1971. (Head of NZ Law Commission)

Lange, David: *Nuclear-Free - the New Zealand Way*; Auckland, 1990

London Nuclear Warfare Tribunal: * Judgment, Report published as *'The Bomb on Trial'*; Swedish Lawyers Against Nuclear Arms/Myrdal Foundation, Munkbron 11, S-111 28 Stockholm, 1989

Mahmassani, S: *Principles of Intl. Law in the light of Islamic Doctrine;* 117 Hague Receuil pp277 ff, 1966

Meyrowitz, Elliott: *The Opinions of Legal Scholars on the Legal Status of Nuclear Weapons;* Stanford J. of Intl. Law, Vol 24,1, 1988

McDougal, Myres and Feliciano, F: *Law and Minimum World Public Order;* New Haven, NY 1961

McDougal, M and Schlei: *The Hydrogen Bomb Tests in Perspective,* 64 Yale Law J, p 648 (1955)

McKee, Alexander: Dresden 1945, *The Devil's Tinderbox;* London 1982

McNair, Arnold: *The Law of Treaties;* London 1961

McWhinney, Edward: * *Course on the World Court at Hague Academy of Intl. Law;* Hague Receuil, 1990

: *The World Court and the Contemporary Law -Making Process;* 1979

: *UN Law-Making;* NY, 1984

Midgley, EBF: *The Natural Law Tradition and the Theory of Intl. Relations;* London 1975

Miller, Arthur S and Feinrider, M (eds): *Nuclear Weapons and the Law;* US, 1984

Morgan, Karl Z: *Hazards of Low-Level Radiation;* in Yearbook of Science and the Future, Supplement to the Encyclopaedia Britannica, 1980

Mothersson, K: *Self-Deterring Orders,* 1991, 20 page paper from author, 53 Victoria St, Kirkpatrick Durham, Castle Douglas, Galloway, Scotland DG7 3HQ

Muller, Hermann: *Radiation and Heredity;* Am Jnl of Public Health, vol 54, 1, 1964 pp 42-50)

Nanda, Ved P and Lowe: * *Nuclear Weapons and the Ecology: Is Intl. Law Helpless to Address the Problem?;* in IALANA Congress papers (above), p 87

Oppenheim, *International Law,* 2 vols, 7th ed by H Lauterpacht, London 1952

Pal, Radhabinod: *Crimes in Intl Relations*; Calcutta, 1955 (main dissenting judge at Tokyo Tribunal)

Pax Legalis: *Papers Indicting UK Government for Conspiracy to Incite Grave Breaches of the Geneva Conventions*; 3 Llys Fammau, Pantymywn, Mold, Clwydd, UK

Pictet, Jean (gen ed): *Commentary on Geneva Conventions,1949*; 4 vols,ICRC,Geneva, 1952-60

: *Commentary on Additional Protocols*, 1977; ICRC, Geneva, 1987

Pogany, I (ed): *Nuclear Weapons and International Law*; Aldershot, UK, 1987

Ramchran BG (ed): *The Right to Life in Intl. Law*; Dordrecht, Netherlands, 1985

Roberts, A and Guelff (eds): * *Documents on the Laws of War*; 2nd ed Oxford 1989 (citations in present text from first edition, 1982)

Rosenne S (ed): *Documents of the ICJ*, 2nd ed., 1979

Rostow, Eugene: *Disputes Involving the Inherent Right of Self-Defence*, AJIL 81 1987

Sadurska, Romana: *Threats of Force*; 82 Am Jnl of Intl. Law, p 239, 1988

Sastry, KRR: *Hinduism and Intl. Law*; 117 Hague Receuil, p 507, 1966

Schell, Jonathon: *The Fate of the Earth*; NY and London 1982

: *The Abolition*; London, 1984

Schindler and Toman (eds): *The Laws of Armed Conflict*, 3rd rev ed, Hague 1988 (citations in present text from 2nd ed, 1981)

Schwarzenberger, George: *The Legality of Nuclear Weapons*; London 1958

: *Intl. Law as Applied by Intl. Courts*; 2 vols, London 1968

Secretariat of the Fourth Review Conference of the NPT: *Background paper on status of negotiations concerning negative security assurances for non-nuclear states*, NPT/CONF.IV/11, Geneva, June 1990

Sherwin, MJ: *A World Destroyed - The Atomic Bomb and the Grand Alliance*; NY 1975

Sims, Nicholas: *Approaches to Disarmament*; Quaker, Peace and Service; London, 1975

Singh, Nagendra: *Nuclear Weapons and Intl. Law*; 1959
and McWhinney, Edward
: * *Nuclear Weapons and Contemporary Intl. Law*; 1989

Social Philosophy and Policy, *Special Issue on Nuclear Rights/ Nuclear Wrongs*; 1985, vol 3

Spaight, JM: *Air Power and War Rights*, 3rd ed; 1947

St John, Edward: *Criminality of Nuclear Weapons - Response to UK Solicitor General*; Occasional Paper, Parliamentarians Global Action, New York (forthcoming)

Stone, Julius: *Legal Controls of International Conflict*; London 1954

Sturgess and Chubb (eds): *Judging the World*; 1988

Union of Intl. Associations: *Yearbook of Intl. Organisations*; Brussels, annual US State Dept: Statement concerning US withdrawal from *Nicaragua proceedings*; Intl. Legal Materials, Vol 24, 1985

US Lawyers Committee on Nuclear Policy: * *Statement on the Illegality of Nuclear Warfare*, revised edition, NY, 1990

USSR Praesidium Decree: *Compulsory Jurisdiction of ICJ re Six Human Rights Treaties*; Am Jnl of Intl. Law, 83 (1989), p 457

van Boven, Theo: *Fundamental Rights and Nuclear Arms*; IALANA papers (above), p 55

van den Biesen, AHJ and Ingelse, P: *Writ of Summons against the State of the Netherlands on behalf of 20,000 plaintiffs*; Foundation 'Ban the Cruise Missiles', Amsterdam 1986

Walzer, Michael: *Just and Unjust Wars*; Pelican, London/NY 1980

Weeramantry, CG: * *Nuclear Weapons and Scientific Responsibility*; Wolfeboro, New Hampshire, 1987

Weil, Prosper: *Le Judaisme et le Developpement du Droit International*; 151 Hague Receuil p 259, 1976

Weston, Burns et al (eds): *International Law and World Order*; 2nd ed, 1990

Zelter, A, and Bhardwaj, AB: *Snowball - the Story of a Nonviolent Civil Disobedience Campaign in Britain*; Ghandi-in-Action, New Delhi, 1991.

CASES CITED

ICJ Advisory Opinions

Interpretation of Peace Treaties, ICJ Reports [ICJ Rep] 1950

Certain Expenses of the UN, ICJ Rep 1962

Legal Consequences for States of the Continued Presence of South Africa in Namibia, ICJ Rep 1971

Western Sahara, ICJ Rep 1975

Contentious Cases - ICJ

Aegean Sea Continental Shelf, ICJ Rep 1976, 1978

Barcelona Traction, ICJ Rep 1970

Corfu Channel, ICJ Rep 1949

Military and Paramilitary Activities in and against Nicaragua, ICJ Rep 1984, 1986

North Sea Continental Shelf, ICJ Rep 1969

Nuclear Tests, ICJ Rep 1973 (Interim Order), 1974 including joint dissenting opinion by Judges Onyeama, et al. Also ICJ Pleadings 1973/74 (2 vols)

South West Africa, Second Phase, ICJ Rep 1966

SS Lotus, 1927 PCIJ, Ser A, No. 10

Tunis-Morocco Nationality Decrees, 1923 PCIJ, Ser B, No. 4

Lake Lanoux Arbitral Tribunal, 1956; 12 UNRIAA

Naulilaa Arbitration; 2 UNRIAA 1012

Palmas Arbitration, 1928; 2 UNRIAA

Trail Smelter Arbitration, 1938-41, 3 UNRIAA p 1905

War Crimes Trials:

Trial of German Major War Criminals [main Nuremberg Judgment], Part 22, London 1950

Hostages Case, Law Reports of Trials of War Criminals [LRTWC], Vol 8, p 34

Krupp Trial, LRTWC Vol 10, p69

Milch Trial, LRTWC Vol 7, p27

Other:

The Caroline, 2 Moore, Digest of Intl Law (USA/UK incident): 29 British and Foreign State Papers, p1136 at 1138

Barbuit's case, 1735, 25 ER 777 (England)

Operation Dismantle Inc. et al v. The Queen, (Supreme Court of Canada), 18 DLR (4th) 481 (1985)

Shimoda case; 8 Japanese Annual of Intl. Law 212, 1964 (Japan)

CONTACT LIST

(1) LAWYERS ORGANISATIONS

a) Peace oriented :

International Association of Lawyers Against Nuclear Arms (IALANA), PO Box 11589, 2502 AN the Hague, Netherlands.

IALANA Affiliated Organisations and Observers

(updated February 1992)

Australian Lawyers for Nuclear Disarmament,
c/o Mr Edward St-John Halcyon, 40 Alexandra Crescent, Bayview 2104, Sydney.Australia.

Bangladesh Lawyers Association Against Nuclear Arms (B.L.A.A.N.A.)
Mr Abdul Manna Bhuiyan, Supreme Court of Bangladesh, Chamber: AL-AMIN-LAW HOUSE 28/2 A, Toyenbee Circular Road Hotel Motijheel (1st Floor), Motijheel C/A Motijheel Dakha Bangladesh.

Juristen tegen Kernwapens
c/o Lieven Lenaerts, Machtegaalstraat 47, 2008 Antwerpen Belgium.

Juristes contre la Guerre Nucleaire
c/o Mr René Constant, Rue de l'Alloue, 13, 4400 Flémalle Belgium.

International Association of Lawyers of the Commonwealth of Independent States
Mr Sergey Paramonov, c/o Kalinin Prospekt 18, 103885 Moscow, Russia, CIS.

Jurister for Fred
Prof. Ole Krarup, c/o Det Retsvidenskabelige Institut B, Kebenhavns Universitet, Studiestraede 6, 1455 Kobenhavn K-Denmark.

Palestinian Lawyers Union
Mr Jamal Sourani, 4, Ibn El Waleid Midan, D 0991, Poggi / Cairo, Egypt.

Finnish Lawyers for Peace and Survival
Mrs Talvikki Uuttala, PL 245, 00171 Helsinki, Finland.

Juristes contre l'Arme Nucleaire
c/o Mr Nuri Rivoli, 75001 Paris, France.

IALANA section Germany
Mr Peter Becker, Postfach 1169, W-3550 Marburg, Germany.

Indian Lawyers against Nuclear Arms
Mr Jitendra Sharma, c/o 17, Lawyers Chamber, Supreme Court, New Delhi 110 001, India.

Centro di Iniziativa Giuridica contro la Guerra
c/o Mr Joachim Lau, Casa Aiale, I-52010 Salutio, Italy.

Movement of Lawyers for Elimination of Nuclear Weapons (MLEN)
Mr Tatsuya Dohno, c/o Watanabe Law Office, Oshima Building, 4-7-13 Kudan-Minami, Chi-yoda-ku, 102 Tokyo, Japan.

Vereniging Juristen voor de Vrede
c/o Mr N Steynen, Couwenhoven 52-05, 3703 ER Zeist, Netherlands.

New Zealand Lawyers for Nuclear Disarmament
c/o Mr Harold Evans, 53A Hackthorne Road, Christchurch 2, New Zealand.

Norsk Medlemsgruppe IALANA
c/o Mr Fredrik Heffermehl, Miels Juelsgatan 28 A, 0272 Oslo 2, Norway.

Swedish Lawyers against Nuclear Arms
c/o Mr Stig Gustaffson, Brötväg 47, 16139 Bromma, Sweden.

Lawyers Committee on Nuclear Policy
Attn: Mr Peter Weiss, 666 Broadway, suite 610, New York, NY 10012, USA.

Association des juristes de la République Socialists du Vietnam
Mrs Ngo Ba Thanh, 4, Nguyên Thuong Hiên, Hanoi, Vietnam.

Observer:

Institute for Law and Peace
David Head, 17 Herbert Street, London NW5 4HA, United Kingdom.

also:

Mr Marian Mushkat
P.O.Box 17027, Tel Aviv 61170, Israel.

Judges and State Prosecutors for Peace
Ulf Panzer, Nienstedtener Marktplatz 23, 2000 Hamburg 52, Germany.

Lawyers for Social Responsibility
c/o Jack Coop, Osgoode Hall Law School, York University, 4700 Keele St, Downsview, Ontario M3J 2R2, Canada.

Meiklejohn Civil Liberties Institute
Box 673, Berkeley, CA 94701, USA.

Nuclear Age Peace Foundation
1187 Coast Village Rd, Suite 123, Santa Barbara, CA 93108, USA.

Nuclear Weapons Legal Action
207-145 Spruce St, Ottawa, Ont K1R 6P1, Canada.

World Peace Through Law Centre
1000 Connecticut Ave, NW, #800, Washington DC 20036, USA

b) International Law:

Institut du Droit International
22 ave William-Favrem, 1207 Geneve, Switzerland.

International Law Association
Charles Clore Building, Russell Sq, London, UK.

Intl Institute of Humanitarian Law
Villa Nobel, Corso Cavallotti 116, 18038 San Remo, Italy

c) International Organisations:

International Commission of Jurists
109 route de Chene, BP 120, 1224 Chene-Bougeries, Geneve, Switzerland.

Intl Assoc. of Democratic Lawyers
263 avenue Albert, 1180 Bruxelles, Belgium.

Note: both the ICJ and the IADL are well established and would provide addresses of their national sections, affiliates or main contacts in various countries.

Arab Lawyers Union
13 Arab Lawyers Street, Tolombat-Garden City, Cairo, Egypt

Andean Commission of Jurists
285 Los Sauces, San Isidro, Lima 27, Peru

Commonwealth Lawyers Assoc
c/o Law Society, 50 Chancery Lane, London WC2A 1SX

Inter-African Union of Lawyers
43 bld Pinet Laprade, PO Box 1921, Dakar, Senegal

Intl. Assoc. of Judges
Palazzo di Guistizia, Piazza Cavour, 00193 Roma, Italy

Intl. Bar Assoc
2 Harewood Place, Hanover Sq, London W1R 9NB, UK.

Intl. Federation of Women in Legal Careers
Via R Giovagnoli 6, 00152 Roma, Italy

Intl. Federation of Women Lawyers
186 Fifth Ave, New York, NY 10010, USA

Intl. Juridical Organisation
Via Barberini 3, 00187 Roma, Italy

Societe Internationale de Prophylaxie Criminelle
49 bld Port-Royal, 75013 Paris

Union Internationale des Avocats
18 Charles de Gaulle, 92200 Neuilly, France

Union of Arab Jurists
Almansour, PO Box 6026, Baghdad, Iraq

Young Lawyers Intl. Assoc
69 avenue Victor Hugo, 75783 Paris Cedex 16, France

Note: IALANA and all of (b) and (c) have consultative status with ECOSOC.

(2) OTHER WORLD COURT PROJECT SPONSORS

International

International Peace Bureau
41 rue de Zurich, 1201 Geneva, Switzerland

International Physicians for the Prevention of Nuclear War
126 Rogers St, Cambridge, MA 02142, USA

International Nuclear Free Local Authorities Movement
NuclearPolicy and Information Unit, Town Hall, Manchester M60 2LA, UK.

Nuclear Free and Independent Pacific Movement
Pacific Concerns Resource Centre, PO Box 489, Petersham, NSW 2049, Australia.

Women's International League for Peace and Freedom
1 rue de Varembé, 1211 Geneva 20.

World Peace Council
Lînnrotink. 25 A 6, KRS, 00180 Helsinki, Finland.

National

These are numerous and growing, but two key non-legal contacts are:

- **World Court Project - UK**
  67 Summerheath Rd, Hailsham, Sussex BN27 3DR. (coalition of local and national organisations)
- **Peace Movement Aotearoa**
  35 Rata St, Christchurch, New Zealand.

NB. The best up-to-date listing of peace organisations worldwide (including the *Red Cross* and some UN bodies) is the *World Peace Directory*, contained in the invaluable *Houseman's Peace Diary*, published annually in late August and available from:
5 Caledonian Rd, London N1 9DX, UK. Tel: +44-71-837-4473.
1992 prices: £4.95/US$10.95/Aus$12.95 + postage/packing.

Also worth consulting is the *Access Resource Guide*: an International Directory of Information on War, Peace and Security (238pp), 1988, published by Ballinger, Cambridge, Mass, USA, at US$14.95.

This is well-indexed and is especially useful for detailed information on academic and US-based bodies, but it does cover 59 other countries. New edition forthcoming.

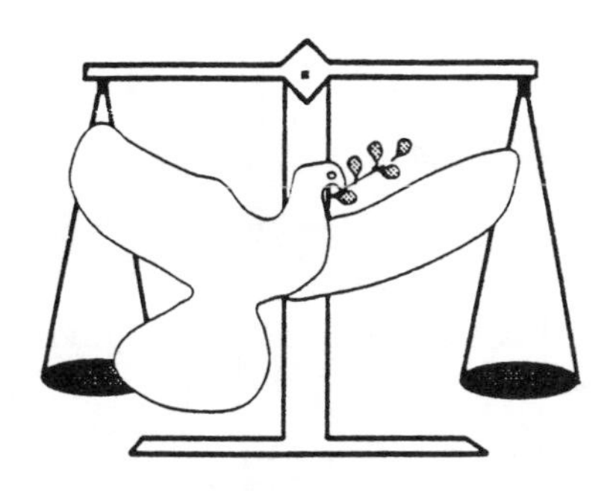

World Court Project - UK Symbol

International Peace Bureau (IPB)

The IPB is a global network of peace activists, with a secretariat based in Geneva, Switzerland. Founded in 1892, it is the world's oldest and most comprehensive international peace movement organisation, bringing together groups of all sizes and types in the common pursuit of the non-violent settlement of conflicts.

Areas of Concern

IPB has consistently emphasised the need to support the disarmament work of the United Nations and to further strengthen international law. At the same time we recognize that grass roots people's movements for peace are of vital significance. Furthermore, peace cannot be separated from the wider issues of economic justice, environmental security and human rights.

In recent years much of IPB's work has been in fields such as nuclear weapons testing and deployment, the arms race at sea, arms transfers and foreign military presence.

Membership

A range of membership types are offered to all independent peace organisations and individuals who share our concerns. Currently we have affiliates from more than 125 organisations in 41 countries on all continents, plus some 100 individuals. Members receive publications and invitations to conferences, have access to our contacts with national missions to the UN and other NGOs, and work together on projects.

Organisation

The Executive Committee, Vice Presidents and other officers are elected by the member organisations at the Annual Assembly. One permanent staff member, the Secretary General, is assisted by an intern provided by Brethren Volunteer Service of the USA and a team of volunteers. We receive donations from members, supporters and foundations, as well as fees and sales income.

History

IPB's early work focused especially on the organisation of Universal Peace Congresses and support for the creation of a League of Nations and a Permanent International Court of Arbitration. For these efforts, and its general work of popularising peace and disarmament issues, the IPB was awarded the Nobel Peace Prize in 1910. In addition, 13 IPB officers have received the Prize as individuals over the years. Since its inception the IPB has organised over 80 seminars and conferences, published reports on international problems and initiated several global campaigns.

Centenary Year: 1992

Since 1992 marks the 100th anniversary of the Bureau's birth, we are planning a number of commemorative gatherings, culminating in a unique, international, multi-forum conference. This will take place 25-30 August in several cities around the Baltic, with a final event in Helsinki. We intend this occasion to be a landmark event, not only for the IPB but also for the wider movement.

How You Can Help

Anyone concerned about international peace and disarmament can make a contribution as:

- member
- donor: gifts, loans, and legacies are all deeply appreciated
- supporter: join or start a national or regional IPB support group
- translator: help needed to publish material in all languages, especially French, German, Spanish, Japanese, Arabic, and Russian
- distributor: local sales agent for IPB literature.

CURRENT ACTIVITIES AND PROJECTS

1. Networking and Servicing

IPB helps to link together many kinds of peace organizations in a variety of ways:

- our annual conference, held in a different part of the world each year, is a major rendezvous for activists and supporters
- seminars are organised on issues of international concern, such as disarmament, environment and devel-opment; the illegality of nuclear weapons; and the aftermath of the Gulf War
- IPB News carries reports from the IPB network, campaign information and an international calendar of events
- IPB is active in promoting and using electronic (computer) communications systems. The IPB secretariat staff runs an electronic conference called 'ipb.news', available on all Association for Progressive Communications systems
- IPB maintains an extensive database of peace organisations from which it can make available labels for mailings.

2. A Peace Movement Link with the United Nations

IPB has had Category II consultative status with ECOSOC since 1977 and is regularly represented at UN and NGO meetings and conferences. These are reported in the 'UN-Watch' section of IPB News, which replaces our former publication Geneva Monitor. IPB is a member of the Geneva Special NGO Committee on Disarmament, among whose current projects is the planning of a conference in 1993 in Katmandu on disarmament and security in the Asia/ Pacific region. Through these meetings, the IPB makes a link with other NGOs and national delegations.

3. Projects

- **World Court Reference Project**: IPB is working with the International Association of Lawyers Against Nuclear Arms, the International Physicians for the Prevention of Nuclear War and other NGOs to secure an Advisory Opinion from the International Court of Justice on the legal status of nuclear warfare.
- **UNCED**: IPB has been active in NGO efforts to ensure that the question of military impact on the environment and development is addressed by the Earth Summit being held in Rio de Janeiro in June 1992.
- **European Peace and Security**: IPB has been active in the creation of a new office in Brussels to monitor the development of European security politics, and is involved in networks such as European Nuclear Disarmament and the Helsinki Citizens Assembly.
- **Arms Trade**: IPB has long supported the work of the European Network Against Arms Trade.
- **Nuclear Proliferation and Testing**: IPB gives general assistance to various initiatives in this increasingly critical area.
- **Conflict resolution**: in the light of the increasing prevalence of ethnic conflicts and the expanding role of the UN, we are considering a study of the ways NGOs can contribute to conflict resolution.
- **Peace History**: in this our centenary year we are undertaking a number of commemorative events, culminating in the Centenary Conference in Helsinki in August.

PUBLICATIONS (prices in Swiss Francs)

IPB News sample 6.00

100 Years of Peacemaking 15.00 - (to institutions) 21.00

Bases and Battleships 4.00

Women and the Military System 20.00

Youth and Conscription 8.00

Children's Campaign for Nuclear Disarmament 4.00

Campaigns Against European Peace Movements 3.00

Tackling the Flow of Arms 15.00 (Available mid-1992)

FACILITIES FOR MEMBERS

Our membership scheme is a way for individuals and groups to both support and be involved in the international network of peace activists, a network linking people in religious bodies, trade unions, women's groups, political parties, green organisations etc as well as simply 'peace' movements.

What we can offer you:

* Regular mailings: IPB News - newsletter of IPB member organisations, with information on peace events all over the world.
* Conference reports and other miscellaneous mailings.
* Access to the Geneva Secretariat and our extensive contacts among Non-Governmental Organisations and national diplomatic missions.
* Lists or labels of peace organisations working in specific fields.
* Invitations to IPB events: seminars, conferences and the Annual Assembly.
* A special on-line electronic conference (computer e-mail) on Association for Progressive Communications networks (PeaceNet, GreenNet, etc.) under the title 'ipb.news'. This carries all our non-book publications and is an information exchange point for all IPB members and supporters.
* Discount rates on IPB book publications.
* The opportunity to work with other IPB members on joint international peace projects.

You can offer us:

* Exchange of information about peace activities in your country/region/field. This could include a regular publications exchange arrangement.
* Financial contributions to help ensure IPB's continuity of work.
* Personal contacts from your own network of friends and colleagues, including potential sources of funding.

The International Peace Bureau